IMMERSION
Bible Studies

LUKE

Praise for IMMERSION

"IMMERSION BIBLE STUDIES is a powerful tool in helping readers to hear God speak through Scripture and to experience a deeper faith as a result."
Adam Hamilton, author of *24 Hours That Changed the World*

"This unique Bible study makes Scripture come alive for students. Through the study, students are invited to move beyond the head into the heart of faith."
Bishop Joseph W. Walker, author of *Love and Intimacy*

"This beautiful series helps readers become fluent in the words and thoughts of God, for purposes of illumination, strength building, and developing a closer walk with the One who loves us so."
Laurie Beth Jones, author of *Jesus, CEO* and *The Path*

"I highly commend to you IMMERSION BIBLE STUDIES, which tells us what the Bible teaches and how to apply it personally."
John Ed Mathison, author of *Treasures of the Transformed Life*

"The IMMERSION BIBLE STUDIES series is no less than a game changer. It ignites the purpose and power of Scripture by showing us how to do more than just know God or love God; it gives us the tools to love like God as well."
Shane Stanford, author of *You Can't Do Everything . . . So Do Something*

IMMERSION
Bible Studies

LUKE

Ron,

God's grace go with
you all the way !

John Indermark

John Indermark

Abingdon Press

Nashville

LUKE
IMMERSION BIBLE STUDIES
by John Indermark

Copyright © 2011 by Abingdon Press

Scripture quotations in this publication, unless otherwise indicated, are from the Common
English Bible, © Copyright 2010 Common English Bible, and are used by permission.

Scripture quotations marked NRSV are from the New Revised Standard Version of the Bible,
copyright 1989, Division of Christian Education of the National Council of the Churches
of Christ in the United States of America. Used by permission. All rights reserved.

Library of Congress Cataloging-in-Publication Data

Indermark, John, 1950–
  Luke / John Indermark.
      p. cm. -- (Immersion Bible studies)
  ISBN 978-1-4267-0983-8 (pbk. : alk. paper)
  1. Bible. N.T. Luke—Textbooks. I. Title.
  BS2596.I53   2010
  226.4'06—dc22
                          2010026841

Editor: Jack A. Keller, Jr.
Leader Guide Writer: Martha Bettis Gee

11 12 13 14 15 16 17 18 19 20—10 9 8 7 6 5 4 3 2 1

Manufactured in the United States of America

Contents

IMMERSION BIBLE STUDIES 7

1. Opening Stories 9

2. Preparing the Way 19

3. Calling Disciples, Forming Community 29

4. Restoring to Wholeness 37

5. God's Character and Reign 45

6. Costs and Joys of Discipleship 55

7. Ascending and Descending Into Jerusalem 65

8. Closing—and Opening—the Gospel 75

Leader Guide 85

REVIEW TEAM

Immersion Bible Studies

A fresh new look at the Bible, from beginning to end,
and what it means in your life.

Welcome to Immersion!

We've asked some of the leading Bible scholars, teachers, and pastors to help us with a new kind of Bible study. Immersion remains true to Scripture but always asks, "Where are you in your life? What do you struggle with? What makes you rejoice?" Then it helps you read the Scriptures to discover their deep, abiding truths. Immersion is about God and God's Word, and it is also about you—not just your thoughts, but your feelings and your faith.

In each study you will prayerfully read the Scripture and reflect on it. Then you will engage it in three ways:

Claim Your Story
    Through stories and questions, think about your life, with its struggles and joys.

Enter the Bible Story
    Explore Scripture and consider what God is saying to you.

Live the Story
    Reflect on what you have discovered, and put it into practice in your life.

IMMERSION makes use of an exciting new translation of Scripture, the Common English Bible (CEB). The CEB and IMMERSION BIBLE STUDIES will offer adults:

- the emotional expectation to find the love of God
- the rational expectation to find the knowledge of God
- reliable, genuine, and credible power to transform lives
- clarity of language

Whether you are using the Common English Bible or another translation, IMMERSION BIBLE STUDIES will offer a refreshing plunge into God's Word, your life, and your life with God.

1.

Opening Stories

Luke 1:1–2:38; 3:23-38

Claim Your Story

We all have to begin somewhere: our first day at school; our first day on a new job; our first child; our first claiming of faith as our own. Consider some of the fears and apprehensions—as well as joys and anticipations—of those first times and others, when a new chapter opened in your life.

Luke has to begin his Gospel somewhere. Like many good storytellers, Luke plants seeds of many themes and emphases that will be consistent throughout this Gospel in these opening stories. Pay close attention to that word *opening*. It's not merely a synonym for "beginning"; it's also an indication of the function of these stories and underlying themes, namely, to *open* eyes and hearts and faith to what may not have been obvious or conventional wisdom to Luke's original audience . . . or to us.

Again, recall those fears and apprehensions, not to mention joys and anticipations, of start-up times in your life and faith. We sometimes enter them with rigid presumptions about how things will be—or how we think they should be! But unless we remain open to what life *really* brings, we may close ourselves off to new experiences and possibilities. Or, in the case of Luke's Gospel, we may close ourselves to God's new ways and presence, revealed in the most unexpected of places and persons and activities.

It's time to open Luke's story—and for Luke's story to open us.

Enter the Bible Story

At the outset, Luke does not tell us about Jesus or John the Baptizer; he tells us about this Gospel he has written. Like the narratives that follow, Luke's first four verses underscore the importance of community. Luke does not only declare that other accounts have already been written; more important, he implies that he is not one of the eyewitnesses "from the beginning" (1:3). In so doing, Luke identifies with every generation of the faithful who have come to rely upon a word passed on. Luke is one of us in his reliance on others to open faith's way. Who have been the ones who opened you to the Christian stories? What moved you to trust and embrace their witness?

Luke offers an even more telling and "opening" detail in these initial verses, which take the form of a prologue similar in style to Greco-Roman histories of that day. Luke identifies this Gospel's recipient: Theophilus (1:3). The name was a common one in Luke's day. Luke's addressing Theophilus as "most noble" may be indicative of someone who has been a patron of this work, either in its creation or its hoped-for dissemination. Another intriguing possibility is that "Theophilus" may not refer to any particular person, but to the shared identity of all those toward whom Luke aims this Gospel. In Greek, *theophilus* means "lover of God" and "beloved of God." Luke's introduction may thus set this Gospel's invitation to all who love, and are loved by, God. Just who are those folks, then and now, and how wide a circle does such love encompass among us? That will be one of Luke's most consistent of concerns and most radical of proclamations.

Context

The sixteenth-century British cleric John Donne penned the memorable line "no man is an island, entire of itself." Life weaves us in a web of connections and relationships, binding us to the times and places and communities in which we live. Even the life of Jesus, unique as it was in some aspects, took place within particular social, historical, and religious contexts that shaped the words and actions by which we have come to know him through Luke and the other Gospels.

Consider that Luke devotes the first half of his Gospel's initial chapter to the appearance of—no, not Jesus, or even Mary or Joseph, but John the Baptizer. The story opens with barrenness, a distinctive signature of several Old Testament birth narratives. Between the lines of all those stories, including Luke's narrative involving John's parents, Elizabeth and Zechariah, is the witness to God as the giver of life. When all seems hopeless, when time seems to have run out, such stories provide their characters, and us, with the potential of life springing out of the very ones life seemed to have passed by. Make no mistake, that is not an easy word or hope to absorb in the midst of such distress. Zechariah, at a loss of faith for such a hope when it comes announced, ends up at a loss for words for the ensuing nine months. Belief does not always come easily. Circumstances can weigh heavily on us, closing us off to any glimpse of change. But remember, Luke's Gospel is about openings. And the opening of Elizabeth's womb initiates this Gospel's insistence on the hope of new life when all seems closed and lost.

Yet another set of contexts takes center stage in Luke's opening chapter, particularly the appearance of the angel Gabriel to the young woman Mary. We hear this passage read most every Advent. But does its familiarity mask this encounter's stunning meaning? Outside of an initial perplexity the angel takes to be fear, Mary conducts herself quite calmly. Mary's sense of openness to it all—to the appearance of an angelic being, to a message and a call no one in the history of the world had ever heard before—surpasses Zechariah's dumbfoundedness at it all.

Above all, Mary is open to entrusting herself to the possibilities of God: "Let it be with me just as you have said" (1:38). Modern-day theories of counseling and leadership lift up the quality of maintaining a "non-anxious presence." Mary embodies that quality in her words and faith. What makes possible the setting aside of anxiety or perplexity is trust that all will be well: "Let it be." Mary's trust makes her the first New Testament disciple in her deep openness to following the "nothing will be impossible" God.

The context of Jesus' life was complex and interconnected long before he took his first breath. He did not stand apart as some isolated island of a figure, his spiritual moorings removed and remote from any and all. So it is with us. Faith is not a distinct compartment of our life; nor are our religious communities and families an isolated sanctuary from the world around us. The gospel is a word and a vocation meant to integrate the whole of our lives. We are as interconnected to one another as we are woven together in God. *Let it be with us just as you have said.*

A Gospel for All

Luke's Gospel opens with a wide array of characters and groups playing vital roles in the stories leading up to and following Jesus' birth. That in itself is not surprising. What is surprising is how many of these people would not have been among the "usual suspects," in that day's wider society, for inclusion—much less elevation—in the company God keeps now and in the coming realm God promises. Their presence here, and later in Luke's Gospel, opens us to a faith that is disinclined to circling the wagons and erecting walls to keep out those who come up short on societal norms of preferred company.

There is, first of all, the central role afforded women in Luke's narrative. New Testament scholar Amy-Jill Levine argues persuasively in *The Misunderstood Jew* that the church has sometimes misrepresented the status afforded women in first-century Judaism. Their standing was far more tenable than that of women in the Gentile cultures of that day. Following that lead, three women in these opening chapters of Luke serve as exemplars of Jewish faith and piety, a theme that recurs later in the case of other women in this Gospel.

Elizabeth appears first. She is not merely the wife of Zechariah. Luke identifies her, with Zechariah, as having priestly ancestry and being "righteous before God" (1:5-6). Beyond that, Luke designates Elizabeth as the first one who is "filled with the Holy Spirit" (1:41; both the Gospel of Luke and Acts, also attributed to Luke, emphasize the movement of God's Spirit). At the end of the birth stories, we encounter another woman: Anna. The first identity Luke attributes to her has nothing to do with her husband (she is widowed) or her children (they are not even mentioned, if there were any). Anna is above all else a prophet (2:36). Additionally, her piety and devotion at the Temple are remarkable. But something else Luke details makes Anna an even more intriguing actor in this Gospel. Simeon had appeared in the story immediately before Anna. He lifted the baby Jesus in his arms, praised God, and spoke to Mary about what would come of this child. But Anna—Anna opened the circle. She began "to speak about Jesus to everyone who was looking forward to the redemption of Jerusalem" (2:38). In other words, Anna was arguably the first apostle in the Gospel—if by "apostle" is meant one who speaks to another about God's saving purposes in Jesus.

A woman who is filled with the Spirit; a woman who is prophetic and apostolic; and as was previously affirmed about Mary, a woman of deep trust whose discipleship opens her to God's purposes for her life: Luke opens us to a Gospel and a community marked by faithful women whose roles are not at all subservient to or dependent upon men. For they are, one and all, reliant upon and revealing of God in our midst.

Mary has another word, a song if you will, that leads this Gospel and us into yet another of its "opening" movements, where inclusion and justice go hand in hand.

Across the Testaments

The Songs of Mary and Hannah

Mary's Magnificat (the name is taken from the Latin for the first word of Luke 1:47-55) blends celebration of God's favor upon her with powerful images of God's favor for the poor and lowly—and with it God's humbling of those in positions of power and privilege. It is a striking song/poem of God's intercession bringing world-transforming reversals of status, where what seem to be future promises are cast in past-tense verbs.

But it is not a new song. In 1 Samuel 2, the once-barren Hannah prays a song/poem in gratitude for the child given to her, whom she has just entrusted to the care of Eli at the shrine in Shiloh. When the songs of Hannah and Mary are held alongside one another, there is remarkable correlation of themes and expressions. In both, the hungry are filled and the lowly are exalted. In both, the powerful are brought down to earth and the privileged are no longer so.

Miraculous births in each case evoke songs of God's power, which overturns business as usual. The songs of these women reflect a truth consistent across the Testaments: God's power and promises will not be turned aside. Things as they are, are not necessarily things as they will be, no matter how entrenched, no matter how pervasive. For with the God who can bring life where life had not been, nothing will be impossible. The songs of these two women are the carols of our hopes.

The community called into being by Mary's song understands God's favor to be more than grace that warms individual human hearts. The favor of God embraces the unfavored in the eyes of the world, and thereby opens community to those otherwise left on the outside looking in. The favor of God likewise overturns the posturing of privilege that self-righteously claims such status as proof of God's favor, and thereby reforms community. That is not just the community Mary opens to us in this song; it is the community Luke comes back to time and again. For whether it is shepherds, who occupied one of the lower rungs of Jewish society, or the gouging tax collector named Zacchaeus, or an unnamed dying thief on a cross, Luke's community is constantly about the inclusion of poor ones or lowly ones, unsavory or seemingly irredeemable ones, the very ones we all presumed had no place or merit. If it is so for Luke's community, how is it so for ours?

There is one final piece to be added about the opening of Luke's Gospel for all. It comes in, of all places, a genealogy. Luke, like Matthew, has a genealogy (3:23-38). There is no exact agreement between them regarding the names, and other such details could be explored. But the chief difference is this: Matthew goes back to Abraham, and shows Jesus to be a son of David and Abraham. Luke has a different perspective in mind. Luke traces Jesus' lineage to David and then Abraham, to be sure—but he keeps going. Luke goes all the way to "son of Adam, son of God." Naming Jesus as the Son of God is surely one of Luke's intentions. But why "son of Adam"? A child of Adam will be kin to every human being—to Israelites and Samaritans, to Jews and Gentiles, to black and white, to prodigals and elders . . . you get the idea. This Gospel opens us to the embrace of God wide enough to sweep up all the children of earth—even the ones we don't get along with; even the ones we disagree with theologically; even the ones whose hymns or political philosophies or lifestyles do not match our own. Why? Because in the beginning, Jesus is the son of Adam, which makes him brother to us all. And if Christ is brother to all, by what presumption do we get to pick and choose who is family and who is not? Is that not God's call in Christ to make?

An Old/New Gospel

In Luke there is distinct continuity between God's established purposes for Israel and the advent in Jesus of God's new purposes. We have seen this already in several ways. Mary sings a song that mother Hannah raised generations before. Jesus' family tree places him squarely in the midst of Israel's stories and traditions. Luke's opening words about why this Gospel identify his purposes at the outset with events "fulfilled among us," hinting strongly at ties with Israel's messianic hopes and prophecies. Luke decides to open not with Jesus' birth but with the Elizabeth/Zechariah narrative that echoes the "barren giving birth" paradigm from the Old Testament.

Other affirmations of Luke's "old/new" Gospel bear repeating for the sake of opening us to the ways in which faith anchors—but does not bury—us in tradition. Mary and Joseph's encounter with Simeon and then Anna comes about because the couple keep the traditions surrounding purification and presentation; yet in keeping ancient tradition, remarkable new words of salvation and decision-making are unleashed.

About the Scripture

Keeping Torah

Jesus' parents raised him in a Torah-observant family. Luke conflates two such traditions kept by Mary and Joseph in their journey to Jerusalem (2:22-24). "Ritual cleansing" (also called "purification"; see Leviticus 12:2-8) referred to sacrifices made in a designated period after birth (a woman was considered unclean for forty days after giving birth to a male child, eighty after a female child). The offering prescribed for this ritual was a lamb or two turtledoves.

The "presenting" of Jesus for "dedication" reflects another Torah tradition regarding firstborn children (Exodus 13:1-2). This traditional upbringing is also reflected in a story about Mary and Joseph taking Jesus to Jerusalem for Passover (2:41-52). There is nothing in Luke or the other Gospels to suggest that Jesus ever ceased to be an observant Jew—a fact that needs to be lifted up whenever anti-Semitism claims Christian faith as an ally.

Before that, Zechariah and Elizabeth keep the ancient tradition of circumcising their child; yet when the time comes to name the child, Elizabeth breaks with tradition by not naming him after his father or another family member: "No, his name will be John" (1:60).

Luke moors his Gospel deeply in the ground of Jewish life and tradition, which is true to the life and ministry of Jesus. But continuity does not always mean conformity. Israel's prophets of old often brought new and transformative words to the community: "Behold, I will create new heavens and a new earth. / The former things will not be remembered, nor will they come to mind" (Isaiah 65:17, New Revised Standard Version); "I will make a new covenant with the people of Israel" (Jeremiah 31:31). So Luke would open us to a Gospel, and a Christ, that is old and new—and ever-renewing of both.

Live the Story

This journey into Luke's Gospel has barely begun, yet already it is beckoning us to open our faith and our communities to the God revealed to us in Jesus.

Just as Luke has written with care about important contexts of Jesus' birth, we are challenged to hold and practice our faith in context. You and I live in particular places and communities. What are the pressing needs for and evidences of hope and new life in your community and in your life? Pray on these two matters: What might a reclaiming of Mary's "nothing is impossible with God" open you to consider or reconsider in your life? What may be holding you back from affirming to God with her, "Let it be with me"?

Luke has given broad hints at a Gospel that will be for all. Who are the ones it is all too easy for you or your faith community to keep at arm's length or to judge? Pray for God's help in making room in your life and in your church for such ones.

As Luke's "old/new" Gospel reveals, we do not come into this story, into our faith journeys, alone or unaided. We come within a tradition—but not in such a way that what has been defines and limits all that will be. What faith traditions do you most value? What do you find most sti-fling? Where do you find the "new" at work in those traditions and in your own spiritual journey?

In light of Luke's opening words and Gospel that seeks to open us, pray to God for the places in your life where you feel the greatest need for opening your heart and mind and spirit to God's ways. And pray with grat-itude for God's all-inviting love revealed in Jesus.

2.

Preparing the Way

Luke 2:39–3:22; 4:1-13

Claim Your Story

Our lives are filled with activities whose outcomes depend on preparation. Cooking, gardening, budgeting, overnight journeys: all need groundwork ahead of time to achieve their intended purposes. So do matters of the heart. How are you preparing your child, and yourself, for that child becoming an independent adult? Or, how are you preparing yourself, and your parent, for a potential reversal of roles when caretakers become the ones in need of caretaking?

On yet another level, readying ourselves for the renewing presence and activity of God in our lives and in all creation involves preparation. What preparations deepen your trust in and service to God? What spiritual groundwork helps keep you and your congregation open to calls of faith that might challenge long-held beliefs and practices?

This chapter's collection of passages from Luke shares a common theme of preparation. Each story relates groundwork laid for God's presence and activity about to unfold in Jesus' life. Growth and faithfulness and ministry do not just happen out of the blue, whether in anticipation of the ministry of Jesus or in our own practice of faithful serving. Preparations must be made for the renewing ways of God. Likewise, preparations are needed for surprises to come on this soon-to-be revealed way, and for adjustments to be made in how life is to be conducted as a result.

Enter the Bible Story

Luke's Gospel bridges the gap between the infant Jesus and the grown teacher poised to enter public ministry with one story set in Jesus' childhood, the only such story related in all four Gospels. Then, in an unnarrated leap of some eighteen years that occurs between the final verse of Chapter 2 and the first verse of Chapter 3, Luke moves on to the narratives of John's ministry and sermonizing, and then to Jesus' temptation in the wilderness.

The preparations evoked within these stories do not end with the biblical characters immediately impacted. Just as Jesus' parents find themselves having to prepare for and adjust to an increasingly independent child, how do we adjust our faith when accustomed relationships and ideas start to change and grow beyond our control? Just as John's ministry to "prepare the way" called people to repentance that clearly addressed public and vocational practices as well as the inner life, how do we prepare for the ways of God that may disrupt once-accepted beliefs and ethical practices? Just as wilderness and testing played prominent roles for John the Baptizer and Jesus, where might we need to go outside the usual and expected places of life and power to discover anew God's providential ways? With such questions, let us enter into narratives that summon our preparations for God's presence and activity in our midst.

Foundations

Sturdiness and rigidity are not always synonyms when it comes to foundations. In earthquake zones, buildings constructed to withstand the ground's shaking and heaving need a certain amount of flexibility to adapt to the motions. Foundations too stiff may crack. On the other hand, the absence of foundations guarantees disaster. A balance must be struck.

Luke leaves no question that Joseph and Mary provided a traditional foundation for their son. They observed the rituals of purification and presentation after Jesus' birth. They made pilgrimage to Jerusalem every year for the Passover. Luke 2:41-51 narrates how those passed-on foundations of faith intertwined with family are tested on one such traditional pilgrimage.

Two assumptions set this testing into motion. Luke tells us that, at Passover's end, Jesus' parents begin the return trip to Nazareth (2:43). Depending upon the route taken, the trip could take anywhere from three days to a week. Jesus is only twelve years old, so Joseph and Mary assume he is with the group of travelers they are journeying with. When they discover he is not, three anxious days of searching follow until at last the wayward son is found at the Temple. In Jesus' response to why he has treated them so comes the story's second assumption: "Didn't you know it was necessary for me to be in my Father's house?" (2:49).

Assumptions can get the best of us in trouble. Luke refrains from providing the parents' reply to their son's rather blunt remark. That Luke does say Jesus returned home and was obedient to his parents may indicate a return to things as they were. But then Luke adds, "His mother cherished [or "treasured"] every word in her heart" (2:51). Her response closely resembles her earlier "treasuring" of the shepherds' words on Jesus' birth night (2:19). Such treasuring suggests something deeper on Mary's part than a *Wow, that was really something!* Mary's considered reflection—better yet, *preparation*—in the wake of the Jerusalem pilgrimage points to her perception of impending changes in the relationship between parent and child.

The boy is still a boy, but not much longer. This youth, whom she once held close to nurse, is starting to have a life of his own. The one whom she once had all to herself now fascinates scribes and priests and teachers. Already, young wings are testing flight. Mary's treasuring of these things about her child is only one verse away from his thirtieth year of life. For Mary, the treasuring becomes prelude for preparing to trust—and entrust—those foundations that she and Joseph laid into the hands of the child so quickly becoming a man.

Such preparations are suggestive of the path to maturity in faith today. We have foundations passed down to us, and likely we have helped construct such foundations for the faith of others. But foundations need testing to see if they have taken root and been owned. When we have been the ones providing those foundations, we need at some point to give others the room and freedom to live and choose and trust (or not) on their own. Life—and church—does not thrive on remaining static, where no one grows or changes or moves on. Mary treasured moments that revealed her child to be something much more than her little boy. In so doing, she prepared for the ministry of—and a new relationship with—her child. We too would do well to treasure experiences that bring such insight into our journeys, preparing us for the unfolding purposes of God, which are apt to bring as much change into our lives and communities as assurance of God's presence in those transitions and transformations.

The other story before us blending foundation and preparation is Jesus' baptism. Luke tells it so briefly that it is unclear whether John is there or not (Luke relates John's imprisonment in 3:19-20 before Jesus' baptism in 3:21-22). The brevity of Luke's baptism account serves to accentuate the threefold affirmation by the heavenly voice as to who Jesus is: Son, beloved, one with whom God is well pleased.

Jesus as Son of God echoes the final line of the genealogy, which follows right after the baptism account. Jesus as the beloved of God indicates the nature of the relationship between God and Christ. Jesus as the one with whom God is well pleased sets a marker down in terms of how God views Jesus—a precursor of how God will view the ministry of Jesus about to unfold. Baptism prepares Jesus himself for ministry by affirming the foundations of his relationship with God. Those foundations prepare Jesus for coming days and conflicts where opponents and finally crucifixion will challenge the validity and trustworthiness of each assertion.

God offers those same foundations to us. We are claimed as God's children most clearly in the sacrament of baptism. We are affirmed as God's beloved, part of the whole God-so-loved world. We are among those with whom God is pleased, for why else would God seek us with grace and favor if all we brought to God were displeasure and revulsion? As with Jesus, these foundations prepare us to live and serve as those so graced and called by God by letting us know who—and whose—we are in preparation for ministry that lives out those identities.

Repentance

John the Baptizer, whose own birth narrative preceded that of Jesus in Luke, prepares the way for God's Messiah. With Matthew and Mark, Luke associates John's ministry with the prophecy of Isaiah regarding a wilderness voice (3:4-6), whose call to prepare God's way offered the theological groundwork for Israel to see a way home from exile in Babylon centuries before.

The other hallmark of John's ministry that Luke shares with the other Gospels is John's preaching a baptism of repentance for the forgiveness of sins (3:3). Ritual washings were a common practice in this era, particularly in the Essene communities around the Dead Sea with which John is often linked. Liturgically, the forgiveness of sins was connected to the sacrificial system in the Jerusalem Temple, particularly the annual Day of Atonement observance. But Essenes and other separatist groups held that Jerusalem and its Temple had become corrupt. This is suggested as one of the chief reasons why such groups withdrew into the Dead Sea region—and why we encounter John's call to repentance not in the Temple courtyard but out in the Jordan wilderness.

About the Scripture

God Works Outside the Usual Boundaries

Luke prefaced the birth story of Jesus by delineating its political and geographical context: when Augustus was emperor in Rome, when Quirinius was governor of Syria, when Joseph and Mary traveled to the town of Bethlehem (2:1-4). Even its Davidic associations could not help Bethlehem from being viewed as a backwater town at this time. It was removed from the religious and political power centered in Jerusalem, and even further removed from that era's focus of all imperial power in Rome.

As Luke now brings John the Baptizer onto the scene to prepare the way for God's *Christ* (the Greek term for "Messiah"), he employs another, more detailed list of how far off the radar this Gospel's events are from the usual centers of power. Read Luke 3:1-2. The word of God comes, not to any in this list's catalogue of contemporary movers and shakers, but to one named John who is in the wilderness. Out in the wild. Away from civilization.

In the musical *Li'l Abner,* the town of Dogpatch is described as "of all the very ordinary most unloved unnecessary places on this earth."[1] That description aptly characterizes where God's word comes to be spoken. Why? To prepare Luke's readers, and Jesus' followers, for the unsettling truth that God works outside the usual boundaries, beyond the conventional wisdoms.

Repentance comes from the Greek word *metanoia*, which literally means "a change of mind." But more than mind, and even heart, are the ethical and societal turnings preached by John. Luke alone among the Gospels provides specifics as to what John's repentance that prepares for God's Messiah entails. To the crowd in general, John commands the practice of sharing with those in need. To tax collectors, John summons a change in what makes their vocations so profitable—and despised—by telling them to collect only what is due and not abuse the system for their advantage. To soldiers, whose wages were notoriously minimal, John counseled abstention from extortion, one of the few ways available to them to profit from their service (3:11-14).

In other words, repentance did not stop with getting one's heart right with God, as if faith could be compartmentalized, separated from the whole of one's life. To prepare for Messiah was to adjust one's social and ethical practices to the values of God's coming Messiah and God's promised realm. In that regard, John stood directly in line with Israel's earlier prophets, who understood that keeping covenant with God invariably went beyond doctrine and ritual. It encompassed life lived with neighbor and stranger, a life that included specific behaviors based on God's vision for human community. Keeping covenant, as Micah 6:8 said of old, truly was doing justice, loving kindness, and walking humbly with God.

John's words continue to call individuals and communities of faith to repentance woven into the practice of daily living. Preparing for God's presence and activity among us today is not window-dressing our sanctuaries with "Welcome home, Jesus" banners. Preparing for God's presence and activity among us, if John is to be trusted, solicits wide-ranging turnings of mind and practices toward such priorities as are revealed in John's proclamation and then Jesus' ministry. Engage in community that shares resources with those in need. Practice vocations in ways that respect others, rather than viewing them as stepping-stones for (or stumbling blocks to) personal advancement or enrichment. And, remembering John's roots in the Essene movement's critique of the Jerusalem establishment, do not hesitate to demand that the community called by Christ's name manage itself by and direct itself toward the qualities and values of our faith, and not by the shortcuts of "what works" in the corporate boardroom or the political think tank. This is God we are preparing for, not what passes for success or prosperity or power on the world's terms—not even when those seductive measures for what represents God's favor are framed by media-savvy religious figures and institutions. Listen for wilderness voices.

Testings and Provisions

The wilderness voice of John has been squelched, in Luke's report, by Herod, embarrassed by John's publicly upbraiding him for his marriage to his brother's wife (3:19-20). But the wilderness setting in Luke continues with the story of Jesus' testing there by yet another wilderness voice, that of a tempter identified by Luke as *diabolos*, "devil" (4:2).

Across the Testaments

Echoes of the Wilderness Experience

The wilderness, John's place of preaching and Jesus' place of testing, had also been of great import in the Hebrew Scriptures. When Israel was carried into exile, the wilderness loomed as an imposing blockade to any hope of return home. Yet Isaiah prepared Israel for exile's end with prophetic imagery of a wilderness transformed by God from an arid, desolate barrier to a watered place with a straight path leading home (35:5-10; 40:3-4). Another foundational story involving the wilderness is that of Israel's deliverance from Egypt, in which freedom came in a wilderness sojourn (see the Book of Exodus).

Jesus' testing in the wilderness strongly echoes the deliverance from Egypt. Testing of both God and people occurred in that older story's narrative. Here the testing involves God (how will God provide for the one just declared beloved?) and Jesus (will Jesus remain faithful to God's purposes, or seek shortcuts?). The connections between Jesus' testing and Israel's wilderness experience become more apparent in the dialogue. Each time Jesus is tested, he responds with Scripture—and each time the quote is from Deuteronomy. Deuteronomy is composed of teachings attributed to Moses that reflect on the wilderness experience and prepare Israel for entrance into the Promised Land. In Luke and the other Gospels, Jesus' time and testing in the wilderness prepare him for an entrance of a different sort: the inauguration of his ministry.

Three temptations are presented to Jesus: to provide food for himself, to receive power (authority) for himself, and to ensure protection for himself. The testings can also be viewed as "shortcuts" to the ministry Jesus is poised to enter. With the turning of stones to bread, the question is: Will his ministry simply be attention-grabbing demonstrations of self-satisfying power? With the receiving of earthly authority, the question is: Will his ministry simply be a quest for privileged authority? With the spectacle at the Temple, the question is: Will his ministry seek to assert first that there will be no risk to self?

Jesus' response to each of the temptations with an appeal to Deuteronomy is revealing in a number of ways. First, Jesus exposes his foundation in Judaism as central to his life and ministry. Jesus is not merely quoting Scripture here; he is grounding his choices and shaping his life's work upon it—and more to the point, upon the God who is revealed in its traditions. What might prepare us to translate and transform our inherited faith into lived priorities? Second, the Book of Deuteronomy powerfully develops the theme of keeping covenant with God as the basis for life and community. The testings posed to Jesus attempt to dissuade him from ultimate allegiance, most clearly by the worship demanded in exchange for the kingdoms of the world. Jesus keeps the covenant tradition that there is no one worthy of worship save God. In what ways do we keep God and Christ central, not in mere lip service or rote recitals, but through lived allegiance, particularly when something is at risk by doing so?

The wilderness testings of Jesus prepare him for ministry in which such temptations and shortcuts will recur. Indeed, Jesus' response to these testings sets the priorities for his ministry.

Where are we tested, and what is at stake? And how do our responses reveal lives and ministries prone to shortcuts . . . or committed to the disciplined keeping of covenant with God and for others?

Live the Story

Every day we prepare for the next, in the choices we make or avoid, in the commitments we keep or neglect, in the relationships we treasure or disregard. Likewise, the life of faith takes shape in the daily decisions and actions whereby we prepare for God's presence and activity in our lives and in the life of this world—or not. In these stories of youthful wing-stretching and repentance-preaching and wilderness-testing, Luke reminds us that the gospel continually calls us to preparations that ready us for the practice of authentic faith.

Look around you—and within you. Where might your faith stand in need of stretching wings to the new and renewing ways of God at work in your heart and within your community? What returning of mind and reforming of ethics and societal engagements might John's preaching of repentance elicit in your life, and for your community? What are the choices facing you that might test whether God is central or peripheral to who you are and what you do as a follower of Jesus and as an active and growing participant in the body of Christ?

Pray about the answers, or further questions, that come to your mind and heart as you reflect on these matters of preparation. And may God bring to you, as God brought to Jesus, such growth and strength and wisdom that comes in receiving and sharing the favor of God.

[1]From *http://www.allmusicals.com/lyrics/lilabner/ragoffenthebush.htm*.

3.

Calling Disciples, Forming Community

Luke 4:14-30; 5:1-11, 27-32; 6:1-49; 7:18-23; 8:1-3; 9:1-6, 18-36

Claim Your Story

The grainy images created by my father's 8-millimeter camera show a procession of children arriving at our home. Some names I remember, some I do not. What I am sure of is that everyone who came had received an invitation to my seventh birthday party. They said yes, and our little two-hour community formed for the sake of games and cake.

Invitations still come to us, no matter our age. Some are for parties or their fellowship equivalents. Others carry more weight. We are invited, but will we respond? Our answer may depend on what we presume will be expected of us, or what we think awaits us. The answer also may hinge on the company of persons we are invited to join. The formation of communities, religious and otherwise, relies on invitations and the responses of those invited to test the waters for themselves.

Luke's Gospel does not tell of Jesus traveling and ministering alone on an empty stage. Words of invitation are spoken by him. Stories of the ones to whom those invitations come, and the words framing what ministry and community may be expected at the end of their "yes," are more than just ancient tales. Through their invitations, we hear our names called to take up Christ's following and vocation. Christ's invitations still come to us: through private moments of devotion; through engagements in worship and service in company with others; through needs etched on the faces of neighbors. The gospel still invites us. What will we say? What will we find at the end of our "yes"?

Enter the Bible Story

The Character of Jesus' Ministry

First words are memorable for a variety of reasons. The first word of an infant in his parents' ears signals a major developmental achievement as an entirely new form of communication begins. The inaugural address of a newly sworn-in president aims to set the tone of hopes and expectations for leadership in the coming term(s). The first sermon of a pastor to her congregation may seek to similarly lay the groundwork for ministry and mission to be undertaken, whether in continuity or breaking with the past.

Luke has provided words spoken by Jesus before he speaks at his hometown synagogue in Nazareth: as a young boy in the Temple, and as a grown man in the wilderness testing. But now, for the first time, Luke offers words that Jesus intones in public ministry for all to hear. Luke's reference to Jesus going to synagogue on the sabbath "as he normally did" (or "as was his custom") underscores the previously noted theme of Jesus' keeping the traditions within which he was raised (4:16). But observing a custom does not necessarily mean doing, or saying, what is customary. Jesus is not there in Nazareth, nor is he here in our lives, to go through the motions of what we all expect him to do or say. Jesus comes as a prophet, for whom ancient words are given fresh, if not always welcomed, interpretation.

The passage found and read by Jesus serves as his "inaugural" for ministry, not only because these are the first public words we hear from him but also because of the way these words point to the character of his ministry about to unfold. Just what are those characteristics of ministry that will be embodied in the coming acts of Jesus' ministry, and that come to serve as a template for the church's ministry in Jesus' name?

"The Spirit of the Lord is upon me" (4:18). Jesus' ministry, and our ministry, is not self-originating or self-empowering. Ministry is grounded in God's Spirit. Both Old and New Testament agree that the Spirit reveals not only God's power—as in the Spirit moving over the waters at creation (Genesis 1:2)—but also God's freedom to go where and to whom God will. In Hebrew and in Greek, the word for "Spirit" is the same as for "wind," and the wind (Spirit) blows where it wills. Where is the power of

Jesus' Prophetic Roots

Jesus' sermon in his hometown synagogue of Nazareth draws heavily upon the Hebrew tradition of prophets—a title and vocation less about future-telling and more about truth-telling. Jesus' "finding" of the passage from Isaiah, whose words he then declares are "fulfilled just as you heard it" (4:21), unmistakably links Jesus with the prophetic theme of hope: hope in the historical context of this passage as return from exile; hope in the developing association of the passage and others like it in Isaiah with messianic expectations.

Another element of Jesus' moorings in the Old Testament prophetic traditions comes in his ensuing comment about prophets not being honored at home (4:24), a reference whose tone is made even sharper in 13:34, where Jerusalem is charged with killing God's prophets. Finally, Jesus accentuates the Old Testament prophetic identity as one who often disturbs the peace when he twice points to prophets (Elijah in 4:26, Elisha in verse 27) whose ministries are exercised outside the "homeland" of Israel. The resulting tumult prefigures the way in which Jesus' prophetic ministry will continue to disturb uneasy peaces —and culminate in attempts to silence his prophetic voice.

God revealed in the church and in your life today? And what does God's "free as the wind" Spirit mean for your journey in faith?

For whose sake is Jesus' ministry exercised? Listen to the list of recipients of Spirit-ed ministry in Jesus' sermon: the poor, the prisoners, the blind, the oppressed (4:18). Those on the underside of life, those routinely overlooked, the vulnerable ones, the ones most often left on the outside looking in: these will be the ones whom Jesus will engage in ministry. Whether in healing or in feeding, in sitting at table with them, or in bringing them into the circle of followers: those who ordinarily go untouched and uncalled will by Jesus be touched and invited in the Gospel of Luke narrates. Who are the ones that the church today, and your congregation, is most eager to touch and call into your community? And to whom might Jesus be eager for you to extend a receptive hand?

What will be extended in Jesus' ministry among such as these? Listen again to the sermon: good news, release, recovery of sight, liberation,

God's favor. Notice these words are not about inducing guilt or giving people only what they deserve. What might the neighbors of your church property point to as "good news" that comes from such proximity to your congregation? What do people hear from—and see in—you that witnesses to a faith more interested in conveying God's favor than impugning blame? What has God freed you from, and what has God freed you for?

Luke's testimony that Jesus' inaugural sermon begins with this extraordinary passage from Isaiah is more than a literary device to prepare us for the kinds of things and sorts of persons engaged in Jesus' ministry. By setting out the core characteristics of his ministry, Jesus invites the church to ministry and mission that carries on his practice. For we are called, and sent, among the very sorts of people Christ ministered to and sat at table with and welcomed into the circle, much to the consternation of that day's religious and moral gatekeepers.

Calling and Empowering Disciples

Among the passages that draw focus in this chapter are a number whose underlying theme is discipleship. Some are "call" stories, whereby individuals are invited to follow Jesus. Some are "empowerment" stories, whereby those called become those instructed and sent out to do the work in which Jesus has been engaged. Still others reflect on who these people are that follow and themselves minister to Jesus.

Two call stories merit special attention. One is that of Simon Peter and the other fishermen, in which a miraculous catch of fish results as they follow Jesus' direction as to where to cast their nets (5:1-11). It may be that we look today on this story with eager longing to have such a miracle accompany or motivate our call to follow—as though it would make our decision as "easy" and obvious as theirs must have been. But keep in mind Peter's initial response: his desire to distance himself from Jesus ("Leave me, Lord") is tangled with guilt ("for I'm a sinner"; 5:8). The miraculous overwhelms more than it assures. What clears the way for following him is Jesus' invitation: "Don't be afraid" (5:10). Discipleship is called and empowered first by the removal of fear—fear that stands between us and God, fear that also gets in the way between us as would-be followers and others.

A second call story illustrates Luke's thematic concern with those on the margins who offend not only religious but also moral and even political sensibilities. Luke 5:27-32 narrates not only Jesus' call of the tax collector Levi (often identified with Matthew), but also his table fellowship with those who were that day's counterparts to people you warn your children about associating with, lest reputations be spoiled. Many at that time judged tax collectors to be traitors to their land and people by their very work. What they did provided the means by which Rome extracted the wealth of conquered people and occupied lands. Compounding the fault of calling a tax collector was Jesus' engaging in table fellowship with Levi's other-side-of-the-tracks companions. Table fellowship was taken seriously in first-century Judaism. To eat with another linked you to them, for good and for ill. To eat with tax collectors and sinners, as the right-thinking Pharisees call Jesus to task for (5:30), was an affront to common decency. Jesus' reminder that he came to call such as these is an unsettling reminder then, and still today, that faith kept in closed circles of "those like us" misses the point of Jesus' ministry and our own calling. For we, like Jesus, are to engage in ministry to and with such people as are likely to raise eyebrows and lower curtains in our day as well.

A critical empowerment story unfolds in 9:1-6. The disciples are not just there to observe, take notes, and be ready for the "exam" once Jesus is raised from the dead. Even in the midst of their "apprenticeship" (the Greek word for "disciple" literally means "one who is taught"), Jesus sends them out to do works of ministry. The sending, however, is not just with good wishes: "He gave them power and authority" (9:1). The disciples of Jesus, then and now, are not left helpless. Power and authority come to us. Again, recall Jesus' inaugural words: "The Spirit of the Lord is upon me." Spirit-ed discipleship is empowered discipleship—empowered for the sake of rendering service in Christ's stead.

Finally, there is one crucial discipleship text from Luke among this chapter's passages: 8:1-3. It is so brief that we may miss its power and potential scandal. It lists women who followed Jesus along with the Twelve. Mary Magdalene leads the list, along with others whose names may not be so familiar. Luke later refers to women present in the post-Crucifixion story (24:1-9), when, by the way, the Twelve were nowhere to be found. But even now, in Chapter 8, Luke affords these women not simply a place in the story, but a ministry in the story. The word translated "provided for" in verse 3 is *diakoneo*, a verb that, when used in reference to males, tends to be translated as "minister." So already in the community Jesus calls and empowers, women play a central—and some would argue, a ministerial—role, affording once more a glimpse into Luke's broadly inclusive view of Jesus' ministry and the community it generates.

Framing the Character of Christian Community

Poor ones and blind ones. Prisoners and the oppressed. Women who minister. Tax collectors. The inaugural address of Jesus in Nazareth and the subsequent practice of his ministry is revealing not only of its character; as that ministry takes shape, so Jesus frames the character of the community who would follow him. Among the most extensive teachings surrounding that community, and setting forth the qualities of God's coming realm for which the church is invited to provide lived evidence, are a pair of sermons recorded by Luke and Matthew.

That lived evidence of God's coming realm is to come through a community whose life together, and life for others, abounds in grace. But that is not as easy a calling as it may seem.

Peter, confronted by the power of God's grace, tried distancing himself from such favor as was symbolized in nets full to overflowing (5:8). His reaction is an ironic echo of Jonah, who responded to God's call to head east to Nineveh by taking the first ship west (Jonah 1:3). We too may find ourselves preferring to maintain our own safe distance from a God who proves so gracious in Christ as to invite the likes of tax collectors and sinners—and us—into community.

Jesus' hometown elders and acquaintances, confronted by the scandal of God's grace in their own Scriptures in the stories of Elijah and Elisha, try to take matters into their own hands and stifle grace by casting its prophet off the nearest cliff (Luke 4:29). That they do not succeed by no means guarantees no further conflicts between those who "circle the wagons" to make sure only the righteous get in, and Jesus' brand of table-

Sermons on Mounts and Plains

Luke 6:17-49 and Matthew 5–7 record sermons of Jesus. They have in common teachings about love for enemies and the danger in judging others, and a concluding parable about hearing and doing Jesus' words that uses the contrast of building on rock versus sand (ground). But the differences in the two sermon narratives are far more significant than that of length (Matthew's account is longer by far) or setting (Luke places the teaching on a plain; Matthew, on the side of a mountain).

The chief difference comes in a collection of sayings that, at first glance, seem to be held in common by the two Gospels. These sayings begin "Happy are you . . ." and are sometimes called the Beatitudes. It might appear as though Matthew simply has more. But consider the two passages more closely. In Matthew, the blessings are for the "poor in spirit" and those who "hunger and thirst for righteousness" (5:3, 6). In Luke, it is simply the poor and the hungry who are blessed (6:20-21). Luke's beatitudes reflect Jesus' marked association in this Gospel with the marginalized in life. Further, Luke, unlike Matthew, adds a series of woes: "How terrible for you . . ." Those warned parallel the ones whom Mary sang about being brought low and humbled in the Magnificat of 1:46-55: the rich, the lofty. In Luke, Jesus' ministry and community reflect a reversal of the accepted order: prodigals are welcomed, sinners are sat with at table, and a thief enters paradise at his dying breath. Grace abounds.

sharing, good news-proclaiming invitations to the least and least likely to find a place in the circle.

Blessings spoken upon the down-and-out, and "how terrible for you's" spoken to the up-and-in, are not likely to win friends in high places. Teaching love of enemy to those who have suffered under Roman oppression may not impress their contemporaries, for whom demonizing opponents and exacting revenge is the preferred method. Not engaging in judgment of those whom everyone knows to be deserving may not be appealing to those who take pride in thinking how fortunate God is to have such upstanding friends as us. The first inklings of the cross may not be a great motivator to those for whom religion is about ensuring all will be well and smooth in life.

Just as these framings of Christian community by Jesus ran counter to much of that day's popular religion and culture, so the community formed and framed by Jesus' ministry remains one called to go against the grain of long-accepted societal norms and entrenched conventional wisdoms. Why? Christ has formed and framed us as a community of grace, to proclaim and embody the transformative news of God's favor.

Live the Story

Invitations still come to us today, including the invitation to follow Jesus—an invitation whose "yes" leads to having lives and communities transformed by practicing the ministry of Jesus. How do we, like the disciples and others of old, respond?

As noted in the introduction to this chapter, our answer partly hinges on what we think is expected of us. Sometimes the church does a disservice by making it seem as though discipleship makes no demands. Have you ever had a nominating committee ask you to serve on some board or committee, saying something to the effect of "Don't worry, there isn't that much to it"? Do such invitations aid, or get in the way of, your discipleship?

Our answer partly hinges on the company into which we find ourselves beckoned. Sometimes the appeal of congregations is that they are filled with people like us, who share similar preferences of worship styles or theologies or political parties. But consider again the community that began to take shape in Jesus' practice of ministry. All sorts of people found their way in, or were given a way in not offered before. How might you, and your congregation, practice such invitational ministry as did Jesus—and to the contemporary versions of the clientele Jesus became associated with?

The gospel invites you to take part in the story, to be part of a living community. Prayerfully consider the call to discipleship as you hear it addressed to you: through these stories of Scripture, in your congregation's life together, and in ministry and service out in the world. Pray that the Spirit of God will be upon you to receive, and to bring, good news of God's favor.

4.

Restoring to Wholeness

Luke 5:12-16, 17-26; 7:1-10, 11-17; 8:22-25, 26-39, 40-56; 9:37-43

Claim Your Story

When we bought our home, the first inside work my wife and I did was to pull up the carpeting in the living room and dining room. Much to our surprise, we found unstained hardwood flooring underneath. For nearly eighty years it had been covered up, unused. We quickly decided to restore the flooring with an oil finish, so that the fir strips could finally be seen and used as they were once intended.

Restoration is a key dynamic in spiritual life and Christian ministry. Our lives, relationships, and communities bear varying needs for such reclamation. The need for restoration may arise from broken or diseased places among or within us. The need for restoration may derive from sin that has driven wedges between us and others, God, and even our selves. Restoration brings wholeness to our lives as individuals—and beyond that, to relationships and communities otherwise jeopardized by what created the need for restoration in the first place. Think about your life and spiritual journey at this point in time. Where do you sense the need for restoring wholeness or connection to God, to others, and to yourself? Where are the broken places inside that cry for a healing and restorative touch? Where and by what means have you experienced such restoration?

Enter the Bible Story

The stories from Luke in this chapter share the common theme of restoration. That undercurrent of unity is important to hold before you, for the stories otherwise bring a wide diversity of characters whose lives are transformed by Jesus' words and touch. Likewise, the particular actions of Jesus through which this restoration to wholeness comes also vary widely. There are healings. There are exorcisms. A storm is stilled. There are raisings of two children to life from death.

Yet another common denominator in these narratives of restoration is inclusion in community. Luke's narrative, and Jesus' ministry, is not simply about what happens to certain individuals in isolation. It is about how Christ's restorative ministry brings these individuals back into the circle of community. In the process, these stories invite and challenge Christian community today to include those once on the outside looking in. So let us first explore the needs for restoration facing these characters in Luke, the estrangements from self and community that find healing and wholeness in Jesus' actions. Their stories point us where and with whom the restorative work of Christ and the church may be needed in our own time and in our own lives.

Estrangements

It has often been remarked that "all politics is local." Just so, there are no generic needs for restoration and wholeness in the Gospels, not to mention in our lives. The broken places are known to us in personal ways. Illness enters our bodies not as a theory of medical knowledge, but as aches in our bones and flutters in our hearts and forebodings in our minds of "what next." Even when we spend much energy trying to convince ourselves or others we are "together," deep down we share pressing needs for restorative work to mend and heal the estrangement in our relationships and communities.

The stories of Luke gathered in this chapter are of very particular people facing very distinct issues in their lives. Between the lines of all these stories is how the ailment or situation threatens them with alienation from the community of which they were once a part. Some of these separations from community were handed down to these characters from the very tradition in which they were raised. "Across the Testaments: At Arm's Length" provides more detailed information regarding the man with leprosy and the woman with the flow of blood. But the other characters face implicit estrangements as well.

At Arm's Length

Leprosy was a much-feared condition in the ancient world. It was not a single disease, but a category of multiple conditions that affected skin tissue. Disfiguration could result in severe cases. While modern medicine understands that the disease is not highly contagious, then it was thought otherwise. Leviticus 14:1-32 demanded separation of those with leprosy from the wider community. They were to live alone or in colonies of similarly afflicted ones as exiles. The man with leprosy encountered in Luke 5:12-16 faced not only the debilitating effects of the disease upon his body, but also estrangement from his society and religious rituals as well.

Similarly, Leviticus 15:25-31 legislated that any woman with a discharge of blood apart from her menstrual cycle would be unclean so long as the discharge continued. This state of "uncleanness" set her apart from others, particularly from the worshiping community. To touch or be touched by such a one risked "transmitting" the status of unclean. So consider the dynamics in Luke 8:43-48. This woman has not simply been dealing with the discharge for twelve years; she has been estranged from physical contact with others and from worship. Her touching Jesus is a risky venture for them both, a risk outweighed by her hope of restoration from illness and isolation.

The man who was paralyzed (5:17-26) lacks the mobility to actively participate in community and likely vocation. The disciples on the boat (8:22-25) feared first, the imminence of death, and second, the power of one who could calm the sea. Such fear threatened alienation not only by drowning but also by bewilderment at what it might mean to be in community with such a one who commands the seas. The Gerasene demoniac (8:26-39) and the epileptic boy (9:37-43) suffered from conditions out of their control that made the former a pariah in his community and the latter a danger to himself. The son of the widow in the town of Nain (7:11-17) and the daughter of Jairus (8:40-42a, 49-56)—both of whom are deceased by the time Jesus shows up—face the ultimate estrangement from relationships and community brought by death.

It may be that, reading these stories today, we wonder what connection we have to the characters, or how their stories of estrangement and then restoration connect to our needs and hopes for wholeness. But consider the undercurrents of contemporary connections to these stories. Leprosy may be all but banished today, yet there are those whose lifestyles or economic conditions cause us to steer clear of them. We are less apt to see demonic possession and more inclined to understand what can happen to people with epilepsy or schizophrenia. But we do understand, and sometimes wrestle with ourselves over, matters and addictions that surpass our ability to control in ourselves or for our loved ones.

And as for the disciples' fears exhibited on the boat? We also may find ourselves overwhelmed by waves piling up on our lives. Perhaps they are waves generated by a once-stable relationship with spouse or child, now pummeled with conflicts. Perhaps they are waves thrust up by job loss or medical crisis. We may find ourselves saying with those disciples in our private devotions (we are usually too polite to express this in our public prayers): "Master, Master, we're going to drown!" (8:24).

If we were well and whole, there would be no need for restoration. But like the man who was paralyzed, we sometimes find ourselves unable to move on our own; we need help. Like the woman with the flow of blood, we have grown weary with all the miracle cures and easy answers that are no answers at all, and we long for something, someone, to right what has been wrong for longer than we can remember. Like the disciples, we feel like we are sinking, and we need a lift. If we were well and whole, there would be no need for restoration. But the gospel truth is, we all have places where we are running on empty, or we're out of control, or we don't know where to turn next. Luke's stories point us in the direction of where restoration may be found—and in the process, where we may find ourselves incorporated into a greater whole and wholeness of relationship.

Restoration to Wholeness

Jesus' ministry of restoration in these narratives is joined in several of the stories to "restorative" acts taken *beforehand* by friends and community. The paralyzed man is brought to Jesus by unnamed friends who go to great lengths. Indeed, it is *their* faith Jesus sees (5:20). The healing of the centurion's servant is preceded by Jewish friends who intercede and vouch for the character of their Gentile neighbor (7:4-5). The widow who grieves her dead son was accompanied and surrounded by a "large crowd from the city" (7:12). Two fathers seek out Jesus on behalf of their children (8:41-42; 9:37-43). These details remind us in our own time that restoration by God may entail our involvement in paving the way and not simply in giving thanks after the fact.

As those who follow the Christ who healed and restored, we are to be on the vanguard of such work ourselves. Sometimes, as in these cases, our calling may be more in the way of *preparing* or leading others to receive such restoration—to intercede for others, to bear the needs of others, when their voices or spirits or bodies may be exhausted or emptied. It also may be that we can become the ones through whom God works to bring such restoration ourselves. Paul's vivid image of the church as the body of Christ reminds us that, by God's Spirit, we at times may serve as the hands and voices through which Christ's restoration is brought to those who are broken or estranged from life-giving relationships and communities.

About the Scripture

Who Are These People?

Gerasene demoniac (Luke 8:26-39). We hear of Galilee with some frequency in the Gospels—but Gerasene? Ancient manuscripts of Luke actually have three textual variants for the city referenced in verses 26-27: Gerasa, Gadara (as in Matthew 8's parallel story), and Gergesa. Luke's designating it as "across the lake from Galilee," along with the detail of the herd of swine rushing off the cliff into the lake, best fits Gergesa, which was situated right on the Sea of Galilee. Gerasa, on the other hand, was some thirty-plus miles southwest of Galilee. All of those locations, however, were in the Decapolis, whose populations were primarily Gentile (unlike Galilee's mix of Jews and Gentiles).

Centurion (Luke 7:1-10). That this individual was Gentile is clear from the story. That he was Roman, however, is an unprovable assumption. Herod Antipas, ruler of Galilee, employed mercenary troops that could have come from a variety of nations. The title *centurion* identifies a rank in Roman military organization, not necessarily a Roman bloodline. The key detail here is not whether the centurion is Roman, but rather Jesus extolling this Gentile's faith above any encountered thus far among his own people.

The restorative work of Jesus in these stories, whether through healings or exorcisms, calming seas or "giving back" children (see below), accomplishes this reclamation of relationships and community for those graced by Jesus' words or touch. The cases of the man with leprosy and the woman with the flow of blood show this in the broader sense of community restored. Once prohibited from participation in community and liturgical life, they receive not only healing from their physical ailments but also the gift of belonging once again. Two of the stories involving children bring the focus for restoration more sharply into personal relationship. The widow of Nain had lost her son in death, while the father of the epileptic boy had lost his son to a power beyond either his or his son's control. Perhaps only a parent who has experienced such loss can fully appreciate what must be going on inside these two parents. But when restoration comes, the texts' language emphasizes the dramatic and joyous nature of that reversal when they speak in both cases of Jesus "giving back" the child to the parent (7:15; 9:42).

What experiences in our lives, or the faith communities we are part of, can we connect to Christ's continuing ministry of restoration among and within us? Where might we have found common ground with the man with leprosy and the woman with the discharge, kept on the outskirts, only to have someone bring us back inside? In what ways have we witnessed or experienced the "giving back" of life or hope once thought to be lost?

Faith and Fear

Two other recurring themes loom large within these passages from Luke: faith and fear. Faith we might have expected, but fear may take us by surprise.

There are some traditions of healing in the church that place extraordinary weight on the faith of the recipient. *If you only have faith*, the logic runs, *you could be healed*. But that logic is not always followed as "cause and effect" in these stories. Jesus commends the faith of the centurion whose servant he heals (7:9). But certainly there is no faith preceding the healing of the Gerasene demoniac. In the case of the paralyzed man, as noted before, it is not his faith but that of his friends that Jesus affirms (5:20). Even in the case of the man with leprosy, his statement to Jesus that "if you want, you can make me clean" (5:12) is less a statement of faith than a gentle challenge to Jesus' purposes (what is it Jesus wants?). In the case of the widow, it was not faith but Jesus' compassion that served as the trigger (7:13).

This diverse witness to the role of faith in healing and restoration invites a certain humility on our part. We cannot force God to act in the ways we choose simply by claiming faith on our side. Faith is not a vaccination against all that might come to us and even against us. Some of the most faithful among us fall prey to cancer and violent death. What faith brings is the assurance of God's presence and love even in the most outrageous of situations. What faith promises is that we are not forgotten but companioned. I recall from some years ago an account of a journalist who went to the healing shrine of Lourdes. He asked one of the priests about the greatest miracle he had ever seen there. While I no longer have the article to check my memory, I believe the priest's answer went something like: *the faith of those who go away without a cure*. Healing and cure are not always the same thing. Wholeness and restoration come to us on this side of the grave, when God's realm still dwells much in promise and hope. Every person whom Jesus healed later died, as we will too. Faith is the gift of living in these times with hope that exceeds them and infuses them with the grace we hold by trust.

But that is not always or even often easy to do, which may account for why the second recurring theme in these passages is fear. Sometimes the fear is neutral, as in being overwhelmed by something that goes beyond human comprehension. Those who witness the healing of the paralyzed man are reduced to saying, "We've seen unimaginable things today" (Luke 5:26). The community who witnessed Jesus' restoring life to the widow's son blended both fear and praise in their response (7:16).

Fear, however, can lead—then as now—into more ominous directions and responses. The neighbors of the now-restored Gerasene demoniac do not celebrate what Jesus had done: they "asked Jesus to leave their area because they were overcome with fear" (8:37). An individual possessed is now replaced by a community possessed—by fear. Communities and nations seized with fear can do strange things, and destructive ones as well. Far too many contemporary conflicts and tragedies trace directly to fear getting out of hand, driving us away from our usual moral compasses to excuse all manner of evil. So perhaps it is not too difficult to see the implicit connection between these stories that evoke faith and fear with the fact that the final passage considered in this chapter is followed immediately by Jesus' teaching of his passion (9:44-45). To borrow from another of the Gospel traditions, fear of Jesus was rationalized into the strategy that it was better for one to die than for the whole nation to perish (John 11:50).

Yet even that twisted logic wrought by fear became a path whereby God's restorative love and grace came to be revealed on an even greater scale. But that is getting ahead of the story. For now, these passages in Luke affirm Christ's ministry of restoration, a ministry entrusted today to those who follow the path and example of Jesus.

Live the Story

Luke brings to us these stories of restoration, where healing brings with it renewed inclusion in communities and relationships. The question is, what will we do in response to them—or put another way, how will we look for the signs, and practice such ministry of restoration in our time?

In this chapter we've explored estrangements facing several characters in Luke who cried out for healing and wholeness. Part of faith's discipline is to open our eyes, ears, and spirits to those cries *among* us today. Who in your family, in your church, in your community needs the gift of restoration? How might you be an instrument in leading them to such grace and healing in body and spirit as a disciple of Jesus? Just as important, part of faith's discipline is to open our eyes, ears, and spirits to those cries *within* us. Brokenness of body or spirit may be closer to us than ancient narratives penned by Luke. They may be our present condition: perhaps too long fled from or denied, perhaps too long suffered alone or in fear.

Pray for God's healing presence in your life, to restore you to wholeness of life.

Pray for God's empowering presence in your life, to equip you to be a servant of Christ's restorative ministry in the circles in which you live.

And prayerfully consider this week: What else might God be seeking to reveal to you through these stories in Luke for the sake of restoration in and through your life?

5.

God's Character and Reign

Luke 11:1-13, 33-36, 37-54; 12:22-34, 35-48; 13:18-30;
14:7-24; 15:1-32; 16:19-31

Claim Your Story

Think of the ideas of God you had as a child. What did God "look like" to you? What did God do—or not do? Consider how those conceptions of God have changed or deepened over the course of your life. How did experiences of great joy or intense sorrow shape the image of God you carry now? One way to reflect on how you view God is to consider what (and who) you pray for. If prayer is conversation of the heart with God, what do you bring to the conversation, and what do you withhold? How do your choices regarding what to pray hinge on what you trust the character of God to be?

Who God is to us also involves where we think God is leading us and all creation. Has God simply set all this in motion, and is now taking a nap out back while we sort it all out? Or does God remain actively concerned for and involved in life and history? What we believe about the future, and God's purposes for it, logically should impact how we live in this present day. In other words, there should be integrity between our hopes and our current practices of faith. In Scripture, and particularly in Luke, this connection takes shape in stories that relate meanings and "practices" of God's kingdom or reign.

Enter the Bible Story

This chapter (and the next) explores passages from the central section of Luke's Gospel. Narratives of infancy and preparation give way at Luke

About the Faith

Kingdom Language

Luke and the other Gospels are filled with teachings and parables about the "kingdom of God" (or "heaven," as in Matthew). *Kingdom* is a word many find limiting today. Its gender-specific connotation (king, as in "male") does not speak to the inclusive nature of God's grace that is a hallmark of Luke. But there is yet another way in which this term may fall short. In Luke's era, the power ramifications of *kingdom* were clear, for kings were the norm rather than the exception. In that setting, "kingdom of God" served well to contrast the qualities and style of power exercised in this world and the nature and purposes of power in God's realm. Today, kingdoms are largely relics considered in history books. To be sure, there are a few monarchies left; but even where they still exist, they no longer carry the weight of absolutism and brute arbitrariness of the kingdoms against which Jesus contrasted the reign of God. As a result, you will find in this chapter and book various expressions for what the CEB translators render as "kingdom of God": God's sovereign realm, God's commonwealth, God's reign, God's rule . . . and, for the sake of tradition or clarity, occasional usage of *kingdom*.

4:14 to Jesus' ministry in Galilee. But Galilee, Jesus' home and that of most of his disciples, is left behind as Jesus determines to go to Jerusalem, a journey that begins at 9:51. What is at stake in that final destination becomes the concern of Jesus' teachings and stories taken up in this chapter: the character of God, the nature of God's kingdom or sovereign realm, and faith's proclamation and embodiment in our lives and faith communities.

Parables of Surprising Growth and Grace

At the core of Jesus' teaching in Luke, and in several of this chapter's passages, are parables. What is a parable? Celtic spirituality speaks of "thin places": physical locations where the boundaries between heaven and earth, sacred and secular, holy and ordinary, seem to dissolve in ways mystical or spiritual.[1] In these places, the natural becomes a window or a lens that brings into view the holy. That is precisely how the parables of Jesus function. Natural elements (mustard seeds, 13:19), ordinary relationships (parent and child or sibling and sibling, 15:11-32), common practices (dining, 14:12-14): all these and other mundane matters are transformed in the parables into vistas that reveal the character of God and/or the qualities of God's sovereign realm. Of particular importance in the parables considered in this chapter are themes of surprising growth and grace, God's love at work in our midst.

As to surprising growth, take the parables of the mustard seed and the woman who "hides" yeast in flour (13:18-21). The difference in size between a seed and a shrub as large as a small tree, large enough to provide nesting space for birds, is immense. Who would have thought such enormous growth could come from such humble beginnings? But notice also in the parable that it is not growth for growth's sake alone; it is growth for the purpose of providing shelter and home to otherwise vulnerable ones. Such is the nature of God's sovereign realm. Likewise, those of you who have made bread know how little yeast is needed to transform a mass of flour. In this parable, the amount of flour involved is a bushel, nearly fifty pounds, enough to feed 150 people. Again, yeast in the flour does not promote growth for growth's sake alone; it is growth for the purpose of feeding to nourish life. Such is the nature of God's reign.

Growth, however, is not the only surprise encountered in Jesus' parables. There is the surprise of a master who may come at an unexpected hour to find out whether servants are prepared or not (12:35-40). There is the O'Henry-like twist of who is to be invited to dinner parties (14:12-14). There is the shock of a father who loves both his prodigal and stay-at-home children (15:11-32). There is the astonishment that not even the dead returned to life will convince some people (16:19-31).

The surprise and even offense of such parables aims to keep every generation of the faithful on its toes when it comes to what we mean by faith and how we practice it. We find in the parables the countercultural assertion that little things—and little ones—bear extraordinary potential for revealing God's kingdom. We find in the parables a breath of fresh air whispering that, in the end, it is not our well-crafted theologies but God's all-surpassing grace that embraces us in a realm both promised and even now present. Perhaps most freeing, and humbling, of all: we encounter in the parables the truth that the reign of God takes shape not only in ways that might otherwise escape us, but also in and for ones whom we might think God has no use for. Tax collectors and sinners, Pharisees and scribes: As it turns out in the parables, God loves both—which is to say, God loves all.

The God We Encounter in Christ

God loves all. The closing word of the previous section on Luke's parables leads us into the opening affirmation of the God we encounter in Christ in Luke. "All" has been there from the very beginning in Luke, ever since the angel surprised shepherds outside Bethlehem with the announcement of good news "for *all* people" (2:10, emphasis added). The "all" of God's grace takes more particular shape and surprising form in several of the passages before us in this chapter. Hospitality is more than inviting friends and families and potential benefactors to your table; Jesus expands the guest list to those who are poor, crippled, lame, and blind (14:12-13). In the parables of Chapter 15, the "all" of God's grace seeks after and embraces lost and missing ones, even those who have gone off wandering on their own volition or in their own ignorance. In the parable of the rich man and Lazarus (16:19-31), the "all" of God's grace includes the ones routinely overlooked and devalued. The character of God in these stories comes through in the all-seeking and potentially all-embracing love and grace of God.

But the character of God is multifaceted. The "all" of grace does not excuse a *do as we please and anything goes* ethic, without thought of consequence to relationship with God. The rich man lands in a far different destination than does Lazarus (16:23). Is this because he ignored Lazarus in life? Is this an illustration of Mary's song for her unborn child, who would pull the powerful down from their thrones and send the rich away empty-handed (1:52-53)? Luke would have us pause and consider the character of God's justice in our own day and lives.

Luke 11:37-54 carries this thought in yet another direction. Jesus rebukes supposed models of piety and religious knowledge. The problem is not heretical theology or ignorance of Torah. More seriously, some religious leaders have allowed religion to become superficial—to become focused on outward observances and petty rules that hinder rather than help people engage in right relationship with God. To listen to Jesus' scathing remarks is to understand that the "all" of God's grace does not look upon hypocrisy and grandstanding with indifference, but with scorn. Luke would have us pause and consider the character of God's covenanting with us, what such covenant truly seeks—and what is just window-dressing. Tithing mints and herbs while neglecting love and justice is the objection here (11:42). What might be a contemporary version of pious superficiality?

The character of God is also revealed in the prayer Jesus teaches to those who would learn to pray (11:1-4). Sometimes we only get as far as God as "father." But there is far more revealed of God's character than that opening word. There is holiness: God is Mystery and Other, yet still opening to relationship with us. God is providential: for bread, for forgiveness. God is One who does not lead us into places that mislead. This is the God to whom Jesus taught us to pray. How do we integrate these aspects of God's character not only into our prayers but also into the whole of our faith?

About the Scriptures

The Lord's Prayer(s) in Luke and Matthew

As is the case with the Beatitudes, both Luke (11:1-4) and Matthew (6:9-13) offer accounts of the Lord's Prayer. Matthew's account is set in the middle of Jesus' extended teaching known as the Sermon on the Mount. Luke's account falls later in Jesus' ministry, and comes in response to a request from his disciples to be taught to pray just as John the Baptizer taught his disciples to pray. Luke's is a shorter version. It omits the linkage of doing of God's will on earth as in heaven, and simply prays for God's ushering in of the kingdom. Omitted also is Matthew's "rescue us from the evil one" following the petition regarding not leading into temptation.

Perhaps the most significant difference is in the very opening. Luke simply begins with "Father," rather than "Our Father." Luke also does not follow the address of God with "who is in heaven" as does Matthew. Is the first omission because "our" could be heard too exclusively (*ours* versus *theirs*)? Is the second because Luke seeks to affirm a God far more in our midst than a God distant in heaven? How might our thoughts on those questions shape our prayers and faith?

Conversations about the character of God are not merely idle talk or philosophical speculation. To confess our understanding of God's character revealed by Jesus moves our lives and practices in specific directions. For if God would be gracious to all, how might that transform the way we treat others we might ordinarily keep at arm's length? If God is just, what does that imply for our practice of ethics and societal engagement? If God cares not a whit for religious hypocrisy, what does that bring to the integration of our lives with our faith, individually and institutionally?

As you might have guessed, all these questions lead naturally—and needfully—into what it then means for us to prepare for the reign of this God whose character we discern in these passages from Luke.

Preparing for God's Reign

Jesus' teachings in these passages regarding the character and coming realm of God bring a variety of emphases.

The parable of the great banquet (14:15-24) and teachings about "kingdom table manners" (14:7-14) strike an invitational tone. God freely bids us into gracious relationship with God and with one another. *Freely* is a key concept there, for as the parable makes clear, we have the freedom to say no. We are still called today, as individuals and churches, to embody such gracious invitation in the ways we open our communities to any who would seek relationship with God—and to do so in a way that allows the response of "no." For without the freedom of "no," the power of "yes" becomes diluted and lost.

Other passages emphasize appropriate preparation for this realm and the God who brings it. The two parables in 12:35-48 stress the need for readiness as well as faithful stewardship of what has been entrusted into our hands in this "interim" time between Christ's proclaiming of God's coming realm and its fulfillment. In another sense, Jesus' critique of the religious leaders in 11:37-54 indicates that such preparation goes far deeper than rote rituals or self-righteous displays of piety. Our own preparations for God's realm—especially those of us who identify with Christ's community—need to take seriously the warnings against faith that only scratches the surface of how we conduct ourselves individually and insti-

Table Imagery and the Kingdom

In Luke's era and in Jewish tradition, to sit at table with another was not merely to partake of a common meal. The hospitality of sharing a common meal reflected a shared relationship. Psalm 23:5 speaks of God as host of a table who welcomes as well as watches over us. Isaiah 25:6-8 joins such hospitality to the hopes of what God's reign fulfilled will bring: a "table" where death is no more, a table for "all peoples." So when Luke offers his parable of God's realm signified in a great banquet (14:15-24), or when Jesus' rebuke of opponents is triggered by his table manners (11:37-39), we ought not to be surprised. Table fellowship and its attendant hospitality are not merely good manners. They are grounded in long-standing traditions that reach into the way Jesus perceives, and teaches about, the nature and call of God's sovereign realm.

tutionally. We too remain called to faithful stewardship of all that has been entrusted into our care and use for the sake of proclaiming and embodying the qualities of God's promised commonwealth.

Yet another vital emphasis in these passages, particularly in 12:22-34 but also in 11:5-13, is trust in God's providence. We do not worry ourselves into the kingdom; we entrust ourselves into God's keeping. This is the bedrock foundation of Jesus' words about not worrying, as well as the basis upon which we may raise our prayer. God hears. God sees. Do you believe that? More important, do you entrust yourself to that?

Woven through these passages, and others before us in this chapter, is the insight of 12:34: "Where your treasure is, there your heart will be too." Some of us—probably most all of us who have the means to acquire this book and read it at leisure in the comfort of a home—need to take that word *treasure* quite literally. Where, and to what purposes, does your treasure go? Faith is surely a heart matter. But if Jesus is right, the stewardship of one's abundance provides a telling indicator of where your faith is placed.

Beyond that, what is it you greatly treasure and value in life? For there too these words of Jesus come into play. Our values and our valuing are likewise critical indicators of where our hearts reside. Consider making a list right now of what you most value in life. Looking back over it, where and how do the things on that list come into play with the affirmations regarding the character of God and the nature of God's sovereign realm that have been made in this chapter?

Preparing for God's reign does not only come in biblical studies or liturgical rites or long-valued traditions. Preparing for God's reign goes to the heart—the heart of who we are, and what we value, and how we engage in stewardship of all that God has provided. Preparing for God's reign invites us into a state of heart and mind and will that takes seriously what the lilies of the field and the ravens can teach us about God's trustworthy providence. These passages in Luke invite us to such lived trust, but they do not coerce us. For the choice, to be of value, must be ours to make. But know this: God's choice has already been made—and its name is grace.

Live the Story

Think back to where this chapter began: the ideas of God you had as a child; your views of God's purposes for the future; the integrity between our hopes and our practices of faith. After reading this chapter and reviewing these passages from Luke, how have those initial thoughts and perspectives been affirmed; been challenged; been the source of fresh perspective?

The character of God and God's reign are not matters, as indicated earlier, of idle discourse or "armchair quarterbacking." Who we affirm God to be directly impacts our view of who we are called to be as those made in the image of God. What we associate with God's reign transforms how we conduct our lives in its light in the midst of a host of other powers and "realms" making claims upon us. As we treasure our faith in this God and this God's now-and-future reign, faith can go to the heart of who we are and what we do and why we hope.

Spend time with God in prayer. Offer praise for those qualities of God you value and affirm. Ask God questions where you have questions about your faith. Open to the ways God would renew your vision of that coming reign, and embolden your witness to and practice of its gracious nature. Above all: Give thanks to the God we encounter in Christ!

[1]From *Parables and Passion: Jesus' Stories for the Days of Lent,* by John Indermark (Upper Room Books, 2006); page 11.

6.

Costs and Joys of Discipleship

Luke 9:46-48, 57-62; 10:1-12, 17-20, 25-37, 38-42; 14:25-33; 18:18-30; 19:1-10

Claim Your Story

I remember the choice very clearly. The St. Louis public school system gave a battery of tests to fourth-graders. Afterwards, my mother and I were invited to meet with a school counselor. The counselor talked about an accelerated-learning program that offered a number of special learning opportunities to participants, and I was invited to enter this program in the coming fall. The catch was, I would need to start fifth grade in another school in another neighborhood, and leave behind some very good friends. Would I stay where I was, with the friends I knew? Or would I enter the program not knowing who my classmates would be? The choice would bring downsides and benefits.

Downsides and benefits, costs and joys: Most of our choices and their resulting paths include both elements. Our weighing those decisions often hinges on whether we perceive the scale tilting more to the cost or joy side in their consequences. Such choices certainly arise in the church, whether in selecting persons for key leadership positions or engaging in a new program of mission or fundraising. Such choices arise in our personal journeys of faith. Where have you experienced the costs and joys of discipleship inseparably joined?

Enter the Bible Story

Teachings and stories of discipleship comprise the passages from Luke considered in this chapter. Overall themes of grace and inclusion of outsiders continue to weave their way through these passages, in which Luke recounts Jesus praising Samaritans and tax collectors for their actions. But as Luke's narrative draws closer to Jerusalem, harder themes come into play as well: Arguments between followers arise, conflicts with opponents continue, and the costs and joys of discipleship are laid out in sharper relief. But what insights does Jesus bring in Luke to this term *discipleship*—and how do they connect to our calls to follow Jesus?

Discipleship: What Are We Talking About?

A disciple is . . . How would you finish that sentence? Who are the ones whose lives serve for you as embodiments of Christian discipleship? Be aware of these "working definitions" you bring to the theme of discipleship. As you do, listen to the ways in which discipleship is described and summoned by Jesus in Luke.

Among this chapter's passages from Luke is one in which Jesus himself explicitly defines what it means to be his disciple: "Whoever doesn't carry their own cross and follow me cannot be my disciple" (14:27). Before the narratives of Jerusalem and the Passion, Jesus gives discipleship a cruciform shape and calling. As scandalous as that definition sounds standing alone, Luke brackets this teaching of Jesus with two other teachings on discipleship, one before and one after the "carry your own cross" word. The latter of those will be taken up later in this chapter. The former comes in verse 26, where Jesus teaches that one cannot be a disciple without *hating* parents, siblings, spouse, children, and even one's own life. Imagine the response if your church's pastor read this Scripture on Mother's Day or Father's Day. Hatred? Of family? How many would be lined up to follow Jesus on that one?

Fred Craddock helpfully points out in his commentary on Luke in the *Interpretation* series that "hate is a Semitic expression meaning to turn away from, to detach oneself from."[1] Jesus' teaching is not a call to despise with vitriol all of these relationships in our lives. It is, however, a call to order (and at times re-order) all of our relationships and our very life in light of the gospel of Christ. Even if one understands "hating" in this more functional role of setting aside, it still is not a call without cost that can

Disciple: Greek Origins and Gospel Insights

In the New Testament, the Greek word we translate as "disciple" is *mathetes*. It literally means a pupil or learner. To be a disciple of Jesus meant, most literally, to be one who assented to learning what the teacher (Jesus) teaches. But as one quickly discovers in Luke and the other Gospels, discipleship is not merely a commitment to learning the ways of Jesus. The call to discipleship inevitably includes the call to service—and among today's passages, the sending of disciples into the wider community.

Another set of linguistic evidence points to discipleship involving far more than a learning exchange between pupil and teacher. In Luke, there are about fourteen references to or about Jesus as teacher. On the other hand, Luke has disciples and others referring to Jesus as "Lord" almost fifty times. "Lord" carries the meaning of one who holds power or authority over another. A disciple in Luke is not simply one who is taught by Jesus, but one who serves under the lordship of Jesus' authority.

be taken lightly. Clearly, that hardness remains in that expression of Jesus we hear (more often than the saying about hatred) about the meaning of discipleship: cross-carrying.

Notice Jesus says in Luke: "carry *their own* cross." We do not need nor are we called to bear the cross of Jesus. That has been borne already. Discipleship is about making choices and engaging in "detachments" that are particular to our lives. No one need walk Gethsemane's path any longer. But there will be times when we will need to decide whether to take paths that come with costs as well as joys. Perhaps it will be the choice of standing with an unpopular other; perhaps it will be the choice of standing against a popular trend in society or in a congregation. In those times, in those choices, discipleship is revealed in our willingness to practice cruciform following.

Discipleship as the willingness to detach or turn away echoes an earlier passage in Luke (9:57-62). Three individuals seek or are asked to follow Jesus. In two of the cases, the following of Jesus is asked to be put on temporary hold until some very honorable and totally understandable good-byes are made. Jesus' eventual reply to both is: "No one who puts a hand on the plow and looks back is fit for God's kingdom." His word there, in some ways just as harsh as the "hating" passage, does clarify one matter. The following of Jesus, discipleship, is a movement forward. Semitic teaching does not shy away from the use of hyperbole or extremes. Here, the hyperbole of rejecting otherwise understandable reasons for delay intends to underscore dramatically the importance of forward movement. Even relationships of great value and meaning can define us by what has been: We have come from this family. We have made these vows. We have these obligations. All well and good. But Jesus' focus here is not on family per se, but on discipleship. And discipleship leads us forward, orienting us to God's promised realm—and then sets us on the way to speak words and engage in works that are to reveal that kingdom's approach in this present day.

Discipleship: Disciplines for the Way

The resemblance of *discipleship* to *discipline* is not coincidental. For a learner to follow the teachings of a particular teacher, to go back to the literal meaning of *disciple*, involves the discipline of listening carefully, questioning, and heeding. But again, the discipleship of Jesus is not limited to information; it is about *formation*: forming one's faith, character, and actions on the basis of Christ's teachings. We have already looked at the discipline Jesus taught of keeping one's eyes set upon what lies ahead if one is to follow Jesus on the path that leads to God's reign. Other passages before us in this chapter lift up similar disciplines for would-be followers.

In 9:46-48, the disciples' following of Jesus is interrupted by an argument: Who is the greatest among them? From the safety of hindsight, we might shake our heads and wonder what was wrong with those people. Then again, arguments about greatness abound among us today within the church on any number of issues. Greatness is, after all, simply a way of speaking about superiority of position or pride of belief. Whose view of interpreting the Bible is "greatest" among us? Whose perspective on divisive social issues do we deem "greatest" among us? Whose brand of economic philosophy or political posturing is promoted as "greatest" for us? Listen to any contemporary squabble or schism in the church, and you will find at the edges, if not square in the middle of it, disputes over who holds the mantle of "greatness" that claims the final word.

Jesus counters the disciples' arguing by taking a child beside him. Note the emphasis Luke makes here: "Jesus took a *little* child." To welcome such a little one, whether "little" in age or community standing or one normally least-welcomed: that is discipleship's greatness. Jesus calls us to the sometimes costly discipline of humility—humility that follows a course more concerned about the presence of vulnerable ones than about promoting our own agenda. What shape might humility take in those contemporary squabbles or schisms mentioned earlier? What form might humility take in the conduct of your life? What joy might humility bring to you and the wider community?

The most prominent discipline of all, love, comes through an encounter that unfolds into a parable (10:25-37). Luke narrates Jesus' encounter with a legal expert with a twist from the other Gospels. In Mark 12 and Matthew 22, Jesus is asked about the greatest of commandments, and he then provides the answer: love of God and love of neighbor. In Luke, the questioner answers his own question about how to obtain eternal life

Across the Testaments

The Great Commandment(s)

When the legal expert answers Jesus' question in 10:26-27, he speaks out of and interprets Torah traditions they both share. The command to love God with wholeness of heart, being, strength, and mind comes from Deuteronomy 6:5. It follows immediately after the so-called *Shema* ("hear") of verse 4, a primal faith confession of Israel ("Our God is the LORD! Only the LORD!"). The one difference between verse 5 in Deuteronomy and the Lukan account is the addition by the legal expert of "mind" to the list of the faculties by which we are to love God. Matthew's account omits "strength" while Mark follows Luke in listing the four. The command to love neighbor as self comes from Leviticus 19:18. The immediate context of that verse suggests "neighbor" is understood to be the people of Israel. Later in the same chapter (verse 34), the call to love is extended to the "alien [sojourner, immigrant] among you." This widening appeal of love's command fits well with Jesus' expanding of "neighbor" in the parable in Luke 10:30-37.

by appealing to those same commandments to love from the Hebrew Scriptures. But *knowledge* of love, which the expert already possesses, is not the endgame in discipleship. So the expert poses yet another question regarding a possible limiting factor on love's reach: who is my neighbor? That is, who am I obligated to love—and, by implication, who don't I have to worry about?

Jesus' parable of the good Samaritan follows. It is a story that certainly breaks down barriers as to whom we are called to love. Beyond that, the story affirms love is more than emotional attachment, or even dispassionate duty—love is compassion and mercy incarnate. The discipline of love, in the light of this parable, is not what we are supposed to do or must do. Love is what we are able to do, freely, with no thought of recompense, whether from the one we love or from the God who seeks our loving action by loving us first. In Christ, we are disciplined to love that is both compassionate and gracious. How might we ever hope to practice such a discipline? "What is impossible for humans is possible for God" (Luke 18:27).

Discipleship: Conflicts and Expectations

What happens when the disciplines of discipleship are practiced? Jesus does not play down the conflicts and costs that may come in these passages from Luke. Then again, neither does Jesus mute the joy brought by discipleship's embrace of God's reign.

In the narrative of the sending of the seventy-two (10:1-12, 17-20), Jesus communicates not only instructions for their mission but also clear words about what to expect. There will be places of hospitable welcome to, and places of inhospitable rejection of, the proclamation and healing signs of God's realm. Discipleship, then and now, does not embrace a Pollyanna view of the world in which only good things happen. Sin is real. Separation from God and from one another is real. To expect otherwise, to expect that our work and ministry will everywhere and by everyone be embraced, is naiveté that can endanger the church by seducing us into thinking that getting into trouble or "disturbing the peace" must mean we are doing something wrong. Not always; and in fact, it may mean we are doing something right.

About the Christian Faith

Dietrich Bonhoeffer

In June 1939, the German theologian Dietrich Bonhoeffer was in the United States, and while here had been offered a post through Union Theological Seminary. The job would have allowed him to remain in the United States, free and safe from the by-now dominating control of Nazism not only over the German state but also the German church. Earlier, in Advent of 1937, he had authored and published what has become a classic of Christian spirituality titled *The Cost of Discipleship*. Perhaps the weight of his own arguments in that book persuaded Bonhoeffer that his place as a disciple was back in Germany, working for the dissident Christian movement called the Confessing Church. Bonhoeffer actively resisted the Nazi regime, leading in 1943 to his arrest and imprisonment. On Sunday, April 8, 1945, immediately after leading a prayer service, Dietrich Bonhoeffer was taken away and hung the following morning. He was thirty-nine years old. Among his final words spoken to a fellow prisoner were these, which give ultimate expression to discipleship's cost and joy: "This is the end—for me, the beginning of life."[2]

Discipleship's costs come to the surface in several of the passages. The story of Jesus' encounter with the rich ruler (18:18-27) narrates how Jesus sets the demands of discipleship even above that day's expectation of keeping Torah: "Sell everything you own and distribute the money to the poor. . . . And come, follow me" (verse 22). Does Jesus set financial divestment as the bottom line for every disciple of every time? If so, churches that hold reserve savings accounts and pastors with sacrosanct pension plans are in serious trouble. Still, this passage and its later judgment upon the wealthy in verse 24 ought to trouble everyone who too easily says that money is not really what Jesus meant here. He really did mean it literally for that individual. And he really may mean it literally for a whole lot of others who place too much trust in their holdings and not enough trust in God to provide. Perhaps another way of stating the principle that underlies Jesus' words is this: whatever you possess that you cannot give up possesses you. Yet in the wake of the disciples' amazement and astonishment at such cost, Jesus quickly adds that whatever discipleship has let go of will be returned many times over (18:29-30). The story of Zacchaeus in

19:1-10 even illustrates how such letting go can itself become an act of joy, making possible restoration and leading, in Jesus' words, to salvation.

This chapter's final look at the costs and expectations of discipleship comes through the lens of Jesus' encounter with Mary and Martha (10:38-42). Both women engage in the actions of a disciple. Martha busies herself in the right and appropriate work of hospitality. Not to have made preparations for a guest would have been an affront. But preoccupation with the meal causes Martha to lose sight of the discipleship of Mary. Remember the literal meaning of disciple: a learner. Mary sat at Jesus' feet, listening to his message. Her actions too are those of a disciple. Jesus does not take Martha to task for her hospitality, but simply for misplaced priorities.

"One thing is necessary," Jesus says (verse 42). Discipleship is about discerning what is the necessary and needful work or word—or in Mary's case, the *discipline* of listening. To be sure, discipleship cannot always listen and be still. Discipleship needs to act and to serve. The grace and wisdom for a disciple is to know what time it is: to listen, to serve; to give up, to take on; to bring peace, to disturb what only masquerades as peace. But in all things, to love with the humility of one who knows the grace of God's love upon them and upon all.

Live the Story

We make choices all the time in life, and live with the costs and joys that follow. Sometimes we had not foreseen what would come of those choices, and are surprised. Sometimes we knew clearly what was in store, and chose because or in spite of them.

These stories about discipleship in Luke remind us that the choices we make as followers of Jesus, individually and as congregations, have consequences as well. Think about a choice facing you in this moment. It may be explicitly religious or spiritual in nature. But even if it isn't, consider the consequences related to your relationship with God and the faith community—and your own personal spiritual journey. What anticipated costs do you see associated with this? What expected joys might be drawing you one way or another? Pray to God for wisdom and discernment in this choice that impacts your following of Jesus as a faithful disciple.

Think also about a choice facing your faith community at this moment. Reflect on the costs and joys you see as potential outcomes. Pray for your community and its discernment of the path before you all. Then pray for God's leading that you may be a faithful participant in the community's discernment—and then in "walking the walk" of disciples following Jesus in trust and love together.

[1]From *Luke* (Westminster John Knox, 1990); page 181.
[2]From *A Testament to Freedom: The Essential Writings of Dietrich Bonhoeffer*, edited by Geffrey Kelly and F. Burton Nelson (HarperSanFrancisco, 1990); page 46.

7.

Ascending and Descending Into Jerusalem

Luke 19:28–22:53

Claim Your Story

There are journeys to be made that we might prefer deferring or declining altogether. As a child, it might be a trip to the dentist or a walk to the principal's office. As an adult, it might be taking a first step toward the friend or family member with whom we are estranged—or a final step away from another or a group whose ways we can no longer abide. We might prefer not having to take such a path because we don't know what lies ahead, or because we know all too well. For the sake of healing, however, or for the sake of integrity in our values, the journey must be made.

We might even speak of such journeys using a word with spiritual connotations: *pilgrimage*. A pilgrimage ordinarily takes us to a place or person invested with special or holy meaning. For those who consciously view such journeys as pilgrimage, it may even be that the "destinations" become secondary to the journey itself. In what ways do you understand your life as pilgrimage? Where, and toward whom, are you now journeying? And how does your faith shape and inform the paths you choose and reject?

Enter the Bible Story

This chapter's extended passage from Luke encompasses the narratives of Holy Week, from Jesus' entry into Jerusalem to his arrest. Jerusalem was the heart of Judaism's sacred geography. Traditionally associated with both Abraham, as the place of Isaac's near-sacrifice, and David, who made it his capital, Jerusalem and its Temple drew Jewish pilgrims for the three great festivals of Pentecost, Tabernacles, and Passover. We know from John 2:13-25 of at least one previous pilgrimage that Jesus made to Jerusalem with his disciples. But now, beginning at Luke 19:28, Luke narrates Jesus' final pilgrimage to the city to keep the Passover with his disciples. An earlier teaching implies that Jesus understood what awaited him there (18:31-34). Yet Jesus journeys forward. Physically, he ascends from the lower altitudes of Judea to the high ridge called the Mount of Olives, and then descends into the city itself. Spiritually, the ascent is marked with praise and expectation, the descent with conflict and betrayal. Such ascents and descents require preparations to be made by faithful pilgrims in Christ's time, and in our own.

Preparations for Pilgrims

The preparations involved in Holy Week range from mundane instructions for securing a colt for the procession and a room for the Passover meal, to more intricate teachings and parables about watchfulness and preparedness in light of coming times. "Pilgrim" serves as a fitting image to describe the disciples so instructed then, and those who would follow Jesus' instructions in the times unfolding before us. For discipleship remains a journey to be made on paths we might not have chosen had it been simply up to us. Such a pilgrimage that follows the path of Christ requires preparations. In the Holy Week passages, they are preparations about times and events to come, sooner and later.

Jesus' prediction of Jerusalem's destruction (19:41-44) immediately follows his entry into the city. The preparation here is stated in negative terms: The people did not "recognize the time of your gracious visit from God." Luke relates that Jesus wept at this. Missed opportunities are always sad occasions—even more so when the opportunity that comes to us is the very presence of God. The city of Jerusalem, the heart of Jewish hopes and worship in this era: Even it cannot stand when opportunities for recognition of God among us are missed. Jesus' lament in effect becomes a parable, inviting our preparation of our lives and communities for the presence of God in whatever form God chooses.

Related to this lament is Jesus' extended teaching about the Temple's (and Jerusalem's) fate in 21:5-28. What preparations are summoned here? For some, this and related texts are the basis for theologies that long for our exit from this troubled world. This passage is full of violence and destruction, not only in Jerusalem but also on earth and across the whole cosmos. Some scholars hear in this passage the voice and experience of Luke's community, as they reflect back on the destruction of Jerusalem by Rome in A.D. 70, following an unsuccessful revolt by the Zealots. Such times, like those reflected in the Book of Revelation, would have been hard and trying to live through, much less retain hope in. Yet that is precisely what this passage aims to accomplish. When all these things take place, when the very world around us seems in shambles and headed for destruction, when the conventional wisdom says "duck and cover," Jesus instead counsels the faithful to stand straight and look up "because your redemption is near" (21:28). Christ prepares us to be a people of hope, even and especially in the most desperate of times. Consider what that word of preparation might call forth from you, and from your congregation, at this point in time. When economies totter, when partisanship in politics and religion grows rancorous and divisive, our calling is not to pull the sheets over our heads and wait for it all to be over. As pilgrims, Christ calls us to hope. To stay alert. To be engaged in the service Christ rendered as a servant among us.

A similar call for preparedness comes in 22:35-38. Interestingly, it follows immediately on the heels of the announcement that Peter, full of bravado, is ready to die with Jesus. Discipleship is not a matter of boasting of our faithfulness; it is a matter of practicing it. Those who wear their faith on their sleeve are not necessarily those most ready to live it out. Jesus' words of preparation in this passage parallel his sending of the seventy (10:4) in terms of listing what they should take so as to travel lightly. Why do you suppose Jesus emphasizes taking so little? And how might such preparations shape pilgrim disciples—and pilgrim communities—seeking to follow Jesus today?

About the Scripture

"Swords"

"Those who don't own a sword must sell their clothes and buy one" (22:36). Jesus had not mentioned the need of a sword when commissioning the seventy (10:1-4). Why now? Many commentators urge that Jesus uses *sword* symbolically to convey the imminence of danger faced in the garden of Gethsemane and what the soon-to-be apostles will face in their mission. Others take the word literally, using it to justify a militant version of Christianity that fights violence with violence. At the very least, it must be remembered that a traveler's sword was only for self-defense. The argument that Jesus does not speak literally here is bolstered immediately when the disciples boast about having two swords already, to which Jesus responds, "Enough of that!" (22:38). The tone suggests that the disciples once again misunderstand Jesus—a misunderstanding that militant versions of Christianity continue to stumble on. That point is strongly underscored when a disciple uses a sword to wound one of those who came to arrest Jesus (verses 49-50). Jesus' words then: "Stop! No more of this!" Jesus' action then: healing the wounded man. Would that Jesus' words and action then be repeated today when the church too easily sides with meeting violence with violence.

Confronting Fears

Fear confronts us in our lives and journeys. Fear may roil just out of sight, twisting words and actions in ways not always evident or connected to their origins in fear. Fear may also boil over in our midst (or in our hearts), justifying all manner of hatred and resentments without any attempt to disguise its vitriol. Fear also marks a number of these passages in Luke, along with conflicts connected to them. As in our experience, fear in these narratives remains at times beneath the surface, between the lines, to be discerned in objections and questions that seek not so much enlightenment as ensnarement. But sometimes fear breaks into the open.

Implicit fear arises in the Pharisees' attempt to silence Jesus' disciples in the procession (19:39-40) and in the Temple authorities' leanings to kill Jesus (19:47-48).

First, what these Pharisees fear is unclear. Perhaps they fear that the praise rendered to Jesus during the procession could undermine their own standing and authority in the eyes of the crowd. Given the crowds swelling Jerusalem's population for Passover, and the heightened vigilance of the bolstered Roman troops during this time in case of trouble, perhaps the Pharisees fear the situation could get out of hand and imperil the city. Perhaps, as seems to be the case with other Pharisees in 13:31-35 who warn Jesus of danger, these Pharisees in Jerusalem actually seek to protect Jesus from others who would not look favorably on such a demonstration. Whatever their fear might be, however, it leads them to try "shushing" the outcry. Have you ever witnessed (or been party to) an effort to avoid trouble by hushing things up, by keeping quiet? It is like a game played with little children, when we cover our eyes and ask, "Where's Bobbie?" Being out of sight (and sound) may *seem* to provide cover, but realities do not go away by ignoring them. Fears cannot be done away with by pretending they are not there. "Sssh" doesn't work, for as Jesus says, the stones themselves would cry out.

Second, after Jesus clears the Temple, the authorities seek to kill him. They seek to—but they leave it at that. Why? Luke doesn't use the word *fear* in these verses, but it is there: "They couldn't find a way to do it because all the people were enthralled with what they heard" (19:48). The Greek word translated "enthralled" is a compound verb that literally means "to hang upon." In other words, the people (and as noted earlier, it is only the disciples who sing praises in Luke) "hang upon" Jesus' words and actions. They focus their attention on him. Remember also that what has transpired between the entry into the city and this passage is the cleansing of the Temple. The people may not have made up their minds about Jesus, but they are following him closely. And the fear of being seen or judged as short-circuiting the people's attention is not a risk the authorities want to take—yet. For fear prefers the shadows, until risks have been cleared. A similar unstated fear of public opinion drives their later discussion with Jesus on the matter of authority (20:1-5), in which Jesus' answering their question with a question of his own leaves them fearing to tip their hand lest they be subject to public questioning or worse.

In several of Luke's other Holy Week passages, fear is not hidden or shadowed at all. It is right out in the open, lurking like a predator waiting for its time to pounce. In 20:9-19, the religious leaders are so offended by Jesus' parable of the tenant farmers that they are ready then and there to arrest him. But they do not: "They feared the people" (verse 19). Later, the cause of the devising of a plan to arrest and kill Jesus with the eventual help of Judas is stated as: "because they were afraid of the people" (22:2). The ensuing detail that the betrayal must come when "the crowds would be absent" makes clear their fear of the crowd (verse 5).

Such an emphasis on fear might seem unduly harsh or bleak. But the truth of the matter is that Jesus' encounters in Jerusalem are rife with fear—and so is our journey as disciples. Fear is not something to be turned aside from or denied, whether in others or in ourselves. Fear is to be confronted with trust in God's reign that will not be deterred, even when the path to promised light leads through shadowed places and fears.

Passover Pilgrimage

According to the work of the biblical scholar Joachim Jeremias and others, the number of pilgrims converging on Jerusalem amounted to several times the resident population; and the residents of Jerusalem are estimated at the time of Jesus to have been around 25,000 people. So in considering the Passover pilgrimage of Jesus, keep in mind he would likely have been among 50,000 or more people converging on the city.[1]

Jerusalem had a limited number of gates in its walls, so it is not out of the question that the procession narrated in 19:29-39 would have been part of a much larger crowd than the disciples and the other followers of Jesus alone (23:49).

It is important to note, however, that Luke specifies that it was the "throng of his disciples" who rejoice, and the disciples whom the Pharisees seek to silence (19:37, 39). This is in contrast to Mark 11 and Matthew 21, whose narratives indicate the whole crowd is swept up in the praises. Is Luke thus indicating that the crowds remain neutral in their assessment of Jesus, waiting to see what will happen, rather than swinging wildly from "Hosanna" in the procession to "Crucify" on Good Friday, as seems the case in Matthew and Mark?

Across the Testaments

The Passover

The Passover commemorates God's deliverance of Israel from Egypt and is initiated in Exodus 12. In that account, each household of the enslaved Israelites was to slaughter a lamb and spread its blood on the doorposts and lintel of the house (12:7). The lamb was then to be roasted for a meal. That night, all the households of Egypt without blood on the doorway were to suffer the death of their firstborn. Those houses so marked were to be "passed over." Exodus 13:1-6 goes on to provide instruction for the Festival of Unleavened Bread, which calls for a seven-day period of eating no leavened bread. The Seder or Passover meal followed a ritual of eating; its "liturgy" consisted of a series of questions asked by the youngest person at the table, the answers to which explained the meal's elements by recalling the Passover story. Of critical importance: The Passover meal was a meal grounded not in God's forgiveness but in God's deliverance. The sacrifice involved was not a sin offering but a sign of God's remembered and anticipated action to free the people from bondage.

Luke's account of the Passover meal itself involves four elements: preparation, the meal at the table, the word of betrayal, and the debacle of the disciples arguing over greatness at a table Jesus explicitly connects to servanthood. The preparation for the meal (22:7-13), as with the preparation of securing a colt for the procession (19:29-35), adds a sense of mystery and inevitability. Had arrangements already been made with the unidentified man with the water jar? The detail serves as a link with Jesus' earlier teaching about his Passion in Jerusalem: that all is unfolding as intended. The meal at the table becomes the "institution" of the Lord's Supper in later Christian theology. The announcement of betrayal in Luke 22:21-23 comes as no surprise to the reader, as Judas's role had been revealed in 22:3-6. What does come through in Luke's account, however, is that Judas was definitely present at the sharing of the bread and cup (verse 21). Once again, Luke includes the outsider—even the one who will betray.

The final element of the Passover table, along with the table's obvious connection to Communion, is its most critical for discipleship. The disciples' argument about who is greatest among them triggers Jesus' teaching about authority and servanthood in Christian community (22:24-27). This account should be required reading in every church dispute regarding the use of power and claims of privilege. "That's not the way it will be with you" has far too often gone unheard when self-vindicating opinions of who is right and who is wrong are staked. "That's not the way it will be with you" has far too often gone unpracticed when decisions about how to organize or evaluate church institutional structures fall lockstep into the values and power schemes of corporate life today, as they once did into those of absolutist rulers in days gone by.

Servanthood is the path of Christ's disciples, individually and as communities. Servanthood is the commitment to seek the good of others. Servanthood is the willingness to recognize and discipline oneself to a higher power than one's own self-interest. Servanthood first asks about the need of another rather than "what's in it for me." Through such servanthood, God still works to bring about Passover's continuing purposes of deliverance and freedom to God's people. Servanthood brought Jesus to Jerusalem and found embodiment in his words and deeds there. Servanthood is thus to mark our journey as pilgrims who live by the example of the One who came as a servant among us.

Live the Story

No matter our age, our station in life, our relationship status, or our political philosophy, we all have journeys and choices to follow. Sometimes it might seem as though the nature of those paths overwhelms our ability to freely choose; a crisis in health, for example, may restrict those options, at least initially. At other times, our values and faith commitments lead us to decisions and crossroads we had not considered until a certain point.

Luke's stories narrate the ascending and descending road that leads Jesus into and through Jerusalem. The paths are not all bright, nor are they easy. But faithful pilgrimage for Jesus, and the disciples who followed, necessitated the journey.

Consider the ascents and descents facing you in your faith pilgrimage. As in Jerusalem, what are the fears you see descending, in yourself and others? How might these narratives guide you on those paths with renewed trust and hope? As in Jerusalem, where do you see the ascent to servant-hood playing out in your life? How might these narratives guide you as you consider or reconsider what it means for you to be a servant? Pray for God's leading and a renewed vision of the hope that forms your pilgrim way.

[1]From *Jerusalem in the Time of Jesus: An Investigation Into Economic and Social Conditions During the New Testament Period*, by Joachim Jermeias (Fortress, 1969); page 84.

8.

Closing—and Opening—
the Gospel

Luke 22:54–24:53

Claim Your Story

"All good things must come to an end." Every one of us has experience with the reality of those words. The best of books have a final page. The most enjoyable of vacations eventually leads to a return home. Such things we can easily accept, and move on. But not all closures can be accomplished so smoothly. A move or a death may bring closure to a cherished relationship. We may find it time to close the door on a career that has run its course or that has been taken away. It may be that growth or conflict will lead us to close the door to participation in some activity or group.

Is there a personal experience of closure still fresh in your memory or looming before you now? What emotions does it elicit? In what ways has your faith impacted—or how might it impact—the way you deal with or seek such closure? And just as important, how might this act of closing lead to an opening into some new avenue of life or faith?

Enter the Bible Story

Recall that the first chapter in this study considered its passages from Luke as "opening" stories—opening not simply because they come at the beginning of Luke, but opening as a statement of their function in the Gospel. They open us to themes and insights that will be further developed. This chapter engages Luke's closing stories, which narrate the sweep of events from Jesus' trial and crucifixion through resurrection and post-resurrection appearances. But just as in our lives, even in these closings of passion and suffering arise the potential of resurrected and Spirit-ed openings to new life.

Luke populates this extended narrative with a host of characters. Some have been familiar companions along this Gospel's way (Jesus, disciples, religious leaders, the women who followed Jesus, the people or crowds). Two individuals suddenly appear to play authoritative roles: Pilate, the Roman governor; and Herod, the ruler of Galilee. Others are caught up into the narrative almost by coincidence: guards, Simon of Cyrene, mourning women, Barabbas, two condemned criminals, Joseph of Arimathea, Cleopas. The words and actions of all these characters serve as the backdrop for how Luke closes his Gospel. Beyond that, however, their stories become teaching moments of how closures can either become deadening in their effects on us and others—or enlivening in the way some doors swing shut in order to reveal others cracking open.

Closures That Deaden

The initial narratives from Luke provide an almost uninterrupted stretch of episodes in which characters engage in words and actions of closure that deny and deaden relationship, dignity, justice, and eventually life.

The door closes on relationship in Peter's threefold repudiation in the courtyard of the high priest as Peter attempts to secure his own safety by distancing himself from the accused (22:54-62). But there is more to Peter's denial than his connection to Jesus. The second accusation posed to the disciple is not about his acquaintance with Jesus, but about Jesus' community: "You are one of them too" (verse 58). Peter's refutation of any such relationship closes himself off from the community who followed Jesus. Have you ever witnessed such a thing? Have you ever considered such a thing? That is, has association not only with Jesus but also Jesus' community led you to backpedal: "Oh, I'm not one of those people"? Closures need not be as dramatic as Peter's to be deadening in their effect: deadening of faith, when it becomes risky or controversial; deadening of connection to community, when it might summon us to stands we might prefer avoiding.

Human dignity and worth are denied when guards taunt and beat Jesus while he is in their custody (22:63-65). It is an old, old story—and a terribly contemporary one as well. These guards are not the movers and shakers, the decision-makers, whose craft and guile in plotting has brought Jesus into their company. They are more than likely ordinary men, just following orders. Orders to detain—orders, perhaps, to demean. Whether they act on their own in their brutality, we do not know. But we do know they act. The ethic of "just do what you're told" is no ethic at all when it comes to brutalizing another human being in word and in violence. Closing oneself off from the God-given worth of another, for whatever cause and in whoever's name, is a downward descent with no redeeming value.

The religious leaders who convene a hearing on Jesus' fate close the door on ordinary requirements of witnesses to reach their decision (22:66-71). Expediency is always a threat to justice, particularly when expedience is levied in the name of Deity. Ironically, Luke's report of this encounter places the faith claims of Jesus as "Christ" and "God's Son" not on the lips of Jesus or his disciples, but his accusers.

About the Scripture

The "Council"

Luke 22:66 tells us that the priestly leaders and experts in religious law brought Jesus before their "council." This assembly of elders in Jerusalem is elsewhere called by its Greek name: *Sanhedrion* or "Sanhedrin." Uncertainties exist as to the exact role of the Sanhedrin at this time in Judaism. Traditionally it was presided over by the high priest, though Luke does not explicitly mention the high priest presiding over the council's interrogation of Jesus. The council would have had blended advisory and legislative duties for the conduct of the Temple and religious life overall in Jerusalem. The limits on its powers would have been whatever the Roman governor chose to hold for his own. Bringing Jesus before Pilate, the Roman governor or procurator, rather than seeking to execute him by stoning on their own authority, may suggest that the council's power to carry out capital punishment was limited at this time.

The closing off of this narrative to any measure of justice in Jesus' trial and judgment proceeds posthaste with two appearances of Jesus before the Roman governor Pilate that sandwich a brief episode in which Jesus is brought before Herod, the ruler of Galilee (who was in Jerusalem at the time). In his first encounter with Jesus, Pilate seeks to close himself to responsibility for rendering justice by passing off the prisoner to Herod (23:1-7). Herod for his part has no interest in justice, but mere curiosity for some wonder to be done. When Jesus does not "perform," Herod ridicules him before returning him to Pilate (23:8-12). In Jesus' second appearance before Pilate (23:13-24), the Roman governor decisively closes the door to justice and orders an innocent man to death.

Again, the narrative, though ancient, rings chillingly true to life. The flight from responsibility is a familiar tactic: The possession of great power is sometimes seemingly best served by having another take the fall for any exercise of that power. Pilate had the authority to overrule unjust demands. Herod had the ability to take interest in and give shelter to a subject of his realm. Even the religious leaders could have acted independently to carry out the execution, even if it was a risk. But at each turn, no one wanted to have the blame fall on them. The leaders fear the people. Pilate weighs the cost of satisfying or crossing the authorities with whom he is uneasily aligned against the more radical elements of Judaism such as the Zealots. Herod—well, Herod seems to be one who prefers dallying with power or its privileges rather than having to be held accountable for its public exercise. In the end, the representative of Rome commands the release of a murderer and the execution of a teacher.

With that, political and religious authorities combine to close this chapter of Jesus' life by inflicting the most severe of capital punishments in that era: crucifixion. One would think—as they surely thought—the matter would be over and done with.

Closures That Enliven

Not all doors close into the darkness of crucifixion in Luke's closing stories. Some doors close so that new words and acts and paths may come.

Even before and in the midst of crucifixion, closings lead to openings, however tentative.

At the very outset, Peter does not only deny; he also cries uncontrollably (22:62). This might seem at first to be his final descent into that night's bleakness. Perhaps. But tears are a sign of recognition of what has been done. And tears, as you may know from experience, can at times become a starting point, a catharsis, that leads to a new way.

Yet another of those tentative "openings" born of closure comes in the procession to Calvary (23:26-27). A bystander named Simon from the African city of Cyrene is seized and forced to carry Jesus' cross. Symbolism spills out of this simple act. An innocent carries the cross of another innocent, an embodied image of Jesus' call to discipleship as cross-bearing.

On the cross, Jesus engages in two decisive acts of opening others to life in the face of death. In what may be an even more radical declaration than Mark 22's and Matthew 27's "My God, my God, why have you left me?" Luke 23:34 reports Jesus' first words from the cross as these: "Father, forgive them, for they don't know what they're doing." To those who perverted justice, to those who drove nails, Jesus opens the door to forgiveness. His second act of opening life comes in response to one who asks to be remembered. To be crucified was a terribly lonely death, extended in time, the body distended upon the wood, likely naked to increase the shame. It was a place where seeing oneself as utterly forgotten would be a common final thought. To one who pleads not to be forgotten, Jesus offers remembrance and more (verse 43).

At the onset of death and its aftermath, further openings come to light, albeit muted. A centurion, one under command of the procurator, has the courage and honesty to proclaim what Pilate feared to say and stand up for: "It's really true: this man was righteous" (23:47). Keep in mind that *righteous* is in its original meaning was not a religious but a judicial word. "Innocent" would be an equally valid translation. There is a saying that all evil requires is for good men (or people) to do nothing. Luke reports that Joseph, a "good man," has the courage to ask Pilate for Jesus' body for proper burial (verse 52). The women who followed Jesus likewise prepare to keep the traditions of burial, refusing to be closed out by fear of reprisal (verses 55-56). All that prevents them is the eve of sabbath, and so they will wait. Until Sunday.

Come Sunday, the openings begin in earnest, when a tomb closed tight by a stone suddenly becomes the sound chamber for utterly unprecedented news: "He isn't here, but has been raised" (24:6)!

From this point forward, a flood of previously closed doors swing open to new vistas and callings. As in the other Gospels, Luke reports that the first witnesses to Easter are not one or more of the Twelve: The first "apostles" (the Greek word literally means "those sent") of resurrection are the women who followed Jesus (24:9-10). Later, two other followers of Jesus leave Jerusalem for a town called Emmaus. In spite of the women's report, Luke reports them journeying with "faces downcast" (24:17). They are joined by one who at first seems a stranger. This companion engages in two acts of "opening" what had been closed. First, on the way, he opens the Scriptures regarding the necessity of Christ's suffering (24:27). Second, when he accepts their invitation to break bread with them, when he blesses and breaks bread and gives it to them, he opens their eyes to the reality of who he is: the risen Jesus (verse 31).

Across the Testaments

Jesus and "the Scriptures"

Luke indicates that Jesus interprets "the Scriptures" both on the road to Emmaus (24:27) and to the gathered disciples (24:44-45). But what comprised "the Scriptures" in Jesus' day? The Emmaus encounter identifies them as "starting with Moses and going through all the Prophets." Other Gospel references to "the Scriptures" are summed up as "the Law and the Prophets" (for example, Luke 16:16; Matthew 5:17). "Law" traditionally refers to the first five books of the Old Testament, attributed to Moses. "Prophets" encompasses the Former Prophets (Joshua, Judges, Samuel, Kings) and Latter Prophets (Isaiah, Jeremiah, Ezekiel, and the twelve Minor Prophets). But what of the other Old Testament books? Judaism did not finally settle on which of those works, categorized as "Writings," would be considered canonical or authoritative until a generation or more after Jesus. But notice Luke's identification of "Scripture" in verse 44: along with Law and Prophets, the Psalms are included. The Psalms had long been part of Israel's worship, some tracing back to the times of the Former Prophets. So while the final consensus remained on what Writings would be canonized, generations of use in worship invested the Psalms with the authority of Scripture in Jesus' time.

Jesus' action of breaking open Scripture and presence is repeated later when he rejoins the rest of the disciples (24:36-49). Christ opens disciples, then and now, to remembrance and recognition for the sake of hope, for the commissioning of witness, and for the promise of power (24:48-49). With that, the Gospel closes—and the era of the church opens—with Luke reporting Jesus' ascension into heaven and the disciples' return to Jerusalem.

Opening to God's Future

It would seem at this point that the Gospel is closed, its narrative complete. But is it? As carefully constructed and intentionally designed as Luke is (remember Luke's intent, revealed in 1:3, "to write a carefully ordered account"), in the end the Gospel leaves any number of doors ajar in these closing stories. It is not that the narratives themselves are incomplete or partial; it is that their invitation and choices thus pass from the characters on the pages to the readers and listeners—that is, to you and me.

Consider, for example, the close of the Easter-morning narrative. The women return with the news. The men consider their report "nonsense" (24:11). But something then happens between the news of resurrection and the ensuing Emmaus-road encounter: Peter runs to the tomb. "Run" makes clear a sense of urgency; but is the urgency because of panic, or hope? That question hangs in the air. On reaching the tomb, he sees only the linen cloth. There is no angelic messenger, only a burial shroud. Can that alone generate faith? If the word of the women cannot be believed, can a cloth, however precious, do the trick? Apparently not, though again Luke leaves matters up in the air. Peter returns home, "wondering what had happened" (verse 12).

Wonder. It is a curious verb (Greek *thaumazo*) in Luke. In 4:22, the hometown people in the Nazareth synagogue are "so impressed" (*thaumazo*) with Jesus, but their "wonder" is not at all belief, as is soon revealed. In 8:25, disciples "wonder" at Jesus' calming of wind and water—a wonder immediately preceded by Jesus asking them, "Where is your faith?" Perhaps most telling, when Jesus rejoins the rest of the disciples after the Emmaus story, Luke reports that after seeing his wounds the disciples "were wondering and questioning" (24:41). The Greek word for "questioning" literally means "to not believe or trust." In other words, *wonder* is not a synonym for *faith*. It may be a prelude to faith; it may pave the way for opening eyes and spirits. Or wonder may be an emotional or spiritual rush that takes one only so far, but no more.

But to *wonder* at Jesus is not the same as *following* Jesus. For Peter, after hearing the women and seeing the empty tomb, wonder becomes a "teetering" between two worlds. On one side is the world as everyone has always known it, where death closes the final door. On the other side is the world testified to by the women, a world opened to unprecedented transformation by "He has been raised." Peter wonders—but will Peter follow?

Into that opening, Luke bids us insert ourselves. Anybody can—as many sometimes do in the Gospel—wonder at Jesus. Anybody can wonder about the future. But the Gospel of Luke asks and invites: who is ready to move from wonder into trust, from emotional and spiritual rushes into disciplined and persistent following? The Gospel closes—and opens—with the narrative of resurrection, because resurrection is all about opening this whole creation and our individual lives within it to God's transforming power. So Luke closes, that we might be opened.

Live the Story

Go back to that experience of closure fresh in your memory—or looming before you—elicited at the outset of this chapter. What difference do these closing stories in Luke bring to that situation? What difference does trust, not simply wonder, in resurrection hope make as you look back and/or ahead at that situation?

In the end, that is the measure of the impact of faith upon life. It is not about which theory of scriptural inspiration we may or may not hold. It is not about which camp of theology we may champion or critique. The impact of faith upon life, how our words and attitudes and conduct are shaped by the stories we hold as Scripture, is what "living the story" is finally about. How have these stories from Luke explored in this book shaped the way you look at your life, the way you look at others? Luke bids us to a faith ready to be surprised by God in unlikely places and persons. Luke invites us to a God whose love and grace are as expansive as to include prodigals and elders, insiders and outsiders. How might you understand and practice discipleship differently because of Luke? Who is God still calling you to be through this Gospel and its stories?

Pray to God for the power promised in 24:49 to enable your following of Jesus. And then, by the grace of God and in light of Luke's Gospel, live the story!

Leader Guide

People often view the Bible as a maze of obscure people, places, and events from centuries ago and struggle to relate it to their daily lives. IMMERSION invites us to experience the Bible as a record of God's loving revelation to humankind. These studies recognize our emotional, spiritual, and intellectual needs and welcome us into the Bible story and into deeper faith.

As leader of an IMMERSION group, you will help participants to encounter the Word of God and the God of the Word that will lead to new creation in Christ. You do not have to be an expert to lead; in fact, you will participate with your group in listening to and applying God's life-transforming Word to your lives. You and your group will explore the building blocks of the Christian faith through key stories, people, ideas, and teachings in every book of the Bible. You will also explore the bridges and points of connection between the Old and New Testaments.

Choosing and Using the Bible

The central goal of IMMERSION is engaging the members of your group with the Bible in a way that informs their minds, forms their hearts, and transforms the way they live out their Christian faith. Participants will need this study book and a Bible. IMMERSION is an excellent accompaniment to the Common English Bible (CEB). It shares with the CEB four common aims: clarity of language, faith in the Bible's power to transform lives, the emotional expectation that people will find the love of God, and the rational expectation that people will find the knowledge of God.

Other recommended study Bibles include *The New Interpreter's Study Bible* (NRSV), *The New Oxford Annotated Study Bible* (NRSV), *The HarperCollins Study Bible* (NRSV); *the NIV and TNIV Study Bibles*, and the *Archaeological Study Bible* (NIV). Encourage participants to use more than one translation. *The Message: The Bible in Contemporary Language* is a modern paraphrase of the Bible, based on the original languages. Eugene H. Peterson has created a masterful presentation of the Scripture text, which is best used alongside rather than in place of the CEB or another primary English translation.

One of the most reliable interpreters of the Bible's meaning is the Bible itself. Invite participants first of all to allow Scripture to have its say. Pay attention to context. Ask questions of the text. Read every passage with curiosity, always seeking to answer the basic Who? What? Where? When? and Why? questions.

Bible study groups should also have handy essential reference resources in case someone wants more information or needs clarification on specific words, terms, concepts, places, or people mentioned in the Bible. A Bible dictionary, Bible atlas, concordance, and one-volume Bible commentary together make for a good, basic reference library.

The Leader's Role

An effective leader prepares ahead. This leader guide provides easy to follow, step-by-step suggestions for leading a group. The key task of the leader is to guide discussion and activities that will engage heart and head and will invite faith development. Discussion questions are included, and you may want to add questions posed by you or your group. Here are suggestions for helping your group engage Scripture:

State questions clearly and simply.

Ask questions that move Bible truths from "outside" (dealing with concepts, ideas, or information about a passage) to "inside" (relating to the experiences, hopes, and dreams of the participants).

Work for variety in your questions, including compare and contrast, information recall, motivation, connections, speculation, and evaluation.

Avoid questions that call for yes-or-no responses or answers that are obvious.

Don't be afraid of silence during a discussion. It often yields especially thoughtful comments.

Test questions before using them by attempting to answer them yourself.

When leading a discussion, pay attention to the mood of your group by "listening" with your eyes as well as your ears.

Guidelines for the Group

IMMERSION is designed to promote full engagement with the Bible for the purpose of growing faith and building up Christian community. While much can be gained from individual reading, a group Bible study offers an ideal setting in which to achieve these aims. Encourage participants to bring their Bibles and read from Scripture during the session. Invite participants to consider the following guidelines as they participate in the group:

Respect differences of interpretation and understanding.

Support one another with Christian kindness, compassion, and courtesy.

Listen to others with the goal of understanding rather than agreeing or disagreeing.

Celebrate the opportunity to grow in faith through Bible study.

Approach the Bible as a dialogue partner, open to the possibility of being challenged or changed by God's Word.

Recognize that each person brings unique and valuable life experiences to the group and is an important part of the community.

Reflect theologically—that is, be attentive to three basic questions: What does this say about God? What does this say about me/us? What does this say about the relationship between God and me/us?

Commit to a *lived faith response* in light of insights you gain from the Bible. In other words, what changes in attitudes (how you believe) or actions (how you behave) are called for by God's Word?

Group Sessions

The group sessions, like the chapters themselves, are built around three sections: "Claim Your Story," "Enter the Bible Story," and "Live the Story." Sessions are designed to move participants from an awareness of their own life story, issues, needs, and experiences into an encounter and dialogue with the story of Scripture and to make decisions integrating their personal stories and the Bible's story.

The session plans in the following pages will provide questions and activities to help your group focus on the particular content of each chapter. In addition to questions and activities, the plans will include chapter title, Scripture, and faith focus.

Here are things to keep in mind for all the sessions:

Prepare Ahead

Study the Scripture, comparing different translations and perhaps a paraphrase.
Read the chapter, and consider what it says about your life and the Scripture.
Gather materials such as large sheets of paper or a markerboard with markers.
Prepare the learning area. Write the faith focus for all to see.

Welcome Participants

Invite participants to greet one another.
Tell them to find one or two people and talk about the faith focus.
Ask: What words stand out for you? Why?

Guide the Session

Look together at "Claim Your Story." Ask participants to give their reactions to the stories and examples given in each chapter. Use questions from the session plan to elicit comments based on personal experiences and insights.

Ask participants to open their Bibles and "Enter the Bible Story." For each portion of Scripture, use questions from the session plan to help participants gain insight into the text and relate it to issues in their own lives.

Step through the activity or questions posed in "Live the Story." Encourage participants to embrace what they have learned and to apply it in their daily lives.

Invite participants to offer their responses or insights about the boxed material in "Across the Testaments," "About the Scripture," and "About the Christian Faith."

Close the Session

Encourage participants to read the following week's Scripture and chapter before the next session.
Offer a closing prayer.

1. Opening Stories
Luke 1:1–2:38; 3:23-38

Faith Focus

Just as the function of these stories is to open the eyes and hearts of Luke's original audience to what may not be obvious, so too can we open ourselves to God's new ways and presence.

Before the Session

Read these stories from Luke, then read Matthew 1 and 2. Note what aspects of the birth story and what characters are included in each Gospel. Bring a full Nativity set to the session. Set aside the figures and set up the stable in a central location.

Claim Your Story

Invite participants to name a new situation they are preparing to face, such as beginning a new job or facing the "empty nest" for the first time. Discuss what apprehensions, fears, joys, or anticipations they have. Ask them to consider a new situation they have faced in the past. What proved to be surprising? What possibilities opened up that they had not anticipated? Encourage the group to consider this study as a time to be opened to God's presence in a new way through encountering the stories Luke tells.

Enter the Bible Story

The Dedication

Ask participants to tell when they first remember hearing the Christmas story. In what ways did those who told the story serve as early faith mentors for them?

The study writer states that Theophilus may not be the name of a particular person to whom Luke is addressing his Gospel but rather may represent the shared identity of all who are loved by God. What person or groups immediately come to mind as being part of this circle of love?

The Surprising Favor of God

In Luke 1:5-25, 39-80; 2:22-38, the Gospel writer introduces here one of the themes of the Gospel, the central role afforded to women. How do participants respond to the idea of Elizabeth as spirit-filled, Anna as apostle and prophet, and Mary as disciple?

Form two smaller groups. Ask one group to read silently Mary's song (1:46-55) and the other Hannah's song (1 Samuel 2:1b-10). Ask volunteers from each group to alternate reading verses from the two songs. What are the themes that emerge? What is meant by God's favor? Invite someone to read aloud Zechariah's song (1:67-79). What is its focus? What do Mary's and Zechariah's songs reveal about inclusion, and just who will be included?

How does the group see the continuity of Luke's old/new Gospel being revealed? Continuity does not always mean conformity. In what ways are we grounded in the traditions of faith? Where is newness breaking in?

The Breadth of God's Embrace

Ask the group to add to the empty stable those Nativity scene figures that represent characters Luke included in his story. If the group has already studied Matthew, invite them to discuss why Matthew's narrative focuses on the magi. What themes does Matthew's narrative support? How does Luke's story support the theme of inclusion?

Invite the group to compare the genealogy in Matthew 1:1-16 with Luke's in 3:23-38. Form groups of two, with one person in each pair writing down the names in Matthew's list and one Luke's list. What are the differences? How is Luke's perspective revealed here? If through Luke's genealogy he is making the point that Jesus is brother to all and by extension we are all brothers and sisters in Christ, what do participants identify as sticking points for them? What individuals or groups among humankind is it hardest for us to claim as family?

Live the Story

Read aloud Luke 2:1-2. Invite the group to name aspects of the context of first-century Palestine, such as the fact that the people were under occupation, the load of taxation was heavy, and so forth. Then ask them to complete this open-ended sentence: "In our day, in our context . . ." Someone might say "a recession is burdening the people," for example. Then ask them to name places in our context where we are in need of hope and new life. What stands in the way of our opening ourselves to hope and new life? What about our faith tradition grounds us? Until the next session, ask the group to keep the following two questions in their prayers: How can I reclaim Mary's affirmation that nothing is impossible with God? What is holding me back from affirming with Mary, "Let it be with me"?

2. Preparing the Way
Luke 2:39–3:22; 4:1-13

Faith Focus
Luke's stories reveal the groundwork laid for God's presence and activity that were about to unfold in Jesus' life. In our own lives, preparations must be made for the renewing ways of God.

Before the Session
Prepare to lead by opening your heart to the movement of the Holy Spirit and by reading and pondering the Scripture passages and the chapter material. How might participants engage the Bible in ways that inform their minds, form their hearts, and transform the way they live out the Christian faith?

Obtain large sheets of paper and crayons or markers. Ask your pastor for a copy of the baptism liturgy used by your denomination. Read over the words, pondering in what ways you sense that you are beloved of God and a recipient of God's favor. Obtain a clear glass bowl, fill it with water, and place in it clear glass pebbles (available from craft stores).

Claim Your Story
Invite participants to identify a next step they anticipate in their lives, such as a new child, a son or a daughter graduating from high school, an advanced degree, or increased job responsibilities. How are they preparing for this next stage?

Ask the group to identify issues that may represent calls of faith that challenge long-held beliefs and practices—perhaps something as basic as new forms of worship or as complex as who should be ordained or married. What spiritual groundwork helps to keep us open to such calls? What kinds of practices might prepare us for growth and faithfulness? In what ways are we prepared to be surprised by hard insights we might not have welcomed or even expected? What do we do if the required adjustments are not ones we are willing to make?

Enter the Bible Story
The Challenge of Growing
Invite members of the group to listen to this passage from the perspective of Mary or Joseph. Read this passage aloud, stopping at verse 49. What would a parent say to Jesus? As we face changing and growing ideas ourselves, how do we adjust our faith? Does the group agree that sturdiness and rigidity are not necessarily synonyms? How does this apply to raising a child? How does this apply to our faith? How are the foundations of faith tested by changing situations? How can we, like Mary, treasure the foundations of our faith in ways that prepare us to trust the unfolding purposes of God?

Challenge and Confirmation in the Wilderness

Who in our culture might be considered wilderness voices? To what unlikely places might the word of God come? Preparation for the Messiah meant adjusting one's social and ethical practices to the values of God's promised realm. As the study writer says, this preparation is not window-dressing our sanctuaries with "Welcome home, Jesus" banners. Invite participants to suggest what kinds of actions would be appropriate preparation. This might be personal practices or actions the church might take or support. Write those suggestions on the large sheets of paper.

Read aloud the words of institution used in the sacrament of baptism, and consider how God affirms our identity as children of God in baptism. Ask someone in the group to read aloud Luke 2:40 and 2:52, noting that in his younger years, Jesus already revealed he was growing in God's favor. In Jesus' baptism there is a three-fold affirmation: 1) that he is the Son of God; 2) that he is beloved of God; 3) that he is viewed with favor—God is well-pleased with him. In baptism God offers these same foundations to us. How do these foundations prepare us for ministry?

Temptation of Jesus

Invite the group to look up the Old Testament citations to which Jesus refers in this account (Deuteronomy 6:13, 16; 8:3; Psalm 91:11-12). Ask participants to pair up. In each pair, ask one person to consider one of the following from the chapter: What might prepare us to translate and transform our inherited faith into lived priorities? In what ways do we keep God and Christ central through lived allegiance, particularly when something is at risk? Ask them to share their insights with their partner.

Then discuss all together: Where are we tested, and what is at stake? How do our responses reveal lives and ministries prone to shortcuts or committed to disciplined keepings of covenant with God and with others?

Live the Story

Invite the group to consider what "wilderness-testing" experiences they have encountered or expect to encounter. In silence, reflect on the questions at the end of the chapter.

Close by inviting participants to remember their baptisms and to recall the threefold affirmation we receive from God in the sacrament. As each person reaches into the bowl of water and takes a clear glass stone, ask them to pray that these foundations serve to undergird them in the testings of their wilderness experiences.

3. Calling Disciples, Forming Community
Luke 4:14-30; 5:1-11, 27-32; 6:1-49; 7:18-23: 8:1-3; 9:1-6, 18-36

Faith Focus
Jesus Christ invites us into community, calling us to follow him and to lead lives transformed by practicing his ministry.

Before the Session
Obtain invitation cards with the words "You Are Invited." Download and copy short quotes from inaugural addresses of US Presidents such as Abraham Lincoln, Franklin D. Roosevelt, and John F. Kennedy from a site such as *www.presidency.ucsb.edu/inaugurals.php*. Prepare a Venn diagram on a large sheet of paper, sketching out two large circles that overlap with an intersecting space. Check your denominational hymnal for the hymn "The Summons."

Claim Your Story
Hand out the invitation cards to participants. Discuss together what factors influence whether or not they accept an invitation, such as who is extending the invitation or what they are being invited to attend or to do. Ask the group to imagine the invitation they have in hand is coming from Jesus Christ. To what do they think they are being invited? Is there risk involved in accepting this invitation? What will determine how they respond? Does Christ's invitation come to us solely as individuals, or are we invited to come into community?

Enter the Bible Story
Jesus' Inaugural Sermon
Distribute the copies of the quotes from presidential inaugural addresses. How do the quotes point to the kind of presidency each was intending? Ask a volunteer to read aloud Jesus' "inaugural" sermon in this passage. What marks or characteristics of the Spirit would we expect to see in Jesus' ministry? Where is the power of God revealed in the church today? Invite the group to note who the study writer names as recipients of "Spirit-ed" ministry, and list them on a large sheet of paper. Who are the persons or groups today whom your congregation is most eager to call into community? Does it include those whom Jesus names? List what will be extended to these recipients on a large sheet of paper.

Discipleship
The study writer identifies discipleship as the underlying theme of a number of this session's passages. Divide the group into four small groups or pairs, and assign to each small group one of these passages. Ask them to read their passage and refer to the chapter to identify if the passage is a call story, an empowerment story, or one that reflects on who is following Jesus. Discuss the following: When have you observed the miraculous power of the gospel? What about it engendered fear or discomfort? In our church, are we called to reach out to those just like us; or are we to extend the reach of the gospel to oth-

ers who may make us uncomfortable or put us at risk? How do we embrace the power of the gospel in our common life, and what do we do with that power and authority? In Luke's Gospel, women are not only included, they have a defined ministry. Are there groups of people you might be willing to include in the community but would exclude from specific ministry? Why or why not?

The Sermon on the Plain

Invite half the group to read over Luke 6:17-49 silently while the remaining half reads Matthew 5–7 as well as the chapter material. Label one circle on the Venn diagram "Sermon on the Mount" and the other "Sermon on the Plain." Ask participants to name commonalities about these passages, and write down those aspects in the intersecting area of the circles. List distinctive features of each passage. What themes of Luke's Gospel emerge in his writing?

The study writer states that the lived evidence of God's coming realm is to come through a community whose life together is marked by grace, a calling that is not as easy as it may seem. Under what circumstances might we prefer to distance ourselves from a radically inclusive God? In what ways today is the community that is formed in grace and framed by the ministry of grace called to go against societal norms?

Live the Story

Ask participants to consider when they first joined your congregation. What expectations did they have? To be a part of a group like themselves? To enjoy fellowship and have a strong youth group for their children? Consider what would happen if church membership were to be framed as a challenge to stretch and grow as a disciple of Christ. Discuss the question posed by the study writer: How might our congregation practice an invitational ministry modeled on the ministry of Jesus—and to the contemporary versions of the people with whom Jesus associated?

Close by singing the hymn "The Summons," or read Luke 4:18-19 as a prayer.

4. Restoring to Wholeness
Luke 5:12-16, 17-26; 7:1-10, 11-17; 8:22-25, 26-39,40-56; 9:37-43

Faith Focus
Jesus' restorative ministry points us to where restoration may be needed in our own time and brings us back into the circle of community, healing the estrangement of our relationships and transforming our lives.

Before the Session
Consider the persons in your group. What are the issues and life situations that may be causing estrangement from the community for them? Pray that this session will serve to illuminate how we might prepare ourselves to be agents of restoration for those in our community and those beyond our doors. Gather newspapers or news magazines, scissors, glue, and a large sheet of paper for a collage.

Claim Your Story
Ask a group member to read aloud the first paragraph in the study where the writer recounts his experience restoring a wood floor. Invite participants to name similar experiences of restoration, such as restoring a vintage car or a piece of furniture. What is necessary in order that a full restoration might take place? Are there times when an item cannot be restored to its original condition? Are there times when original condition should not be the goal of restoration? What then might be done?

Invite the group to consider their lives silently and to reflect on the questions about where they have experienced brokenness and restoration. Ask those who are willing to share with the group a response to the final question in this section about where and by what means they have experienced restoration.

Enter the Bible Story
Estrangements
Ask participants to cut headlines, articles, or stories from the newspaper or magazines that show brokenness in our time and attach them to the collage. In these contemporary stories, what brokenness is revealed? Who are the ones on the outside looking in? Who is experiencing estrangement?

Assign to each participant one of the eight stories in this session. Ask them to read the passage, then read over the material in the study that addresses the estrangement laid bare in the story. After a few minutes, suggest that each person pair up with someone who read a different passage, and discuss the estrangement being experienced. As a group, discuss what other contemporary parallels to stories or situations can be suggested. With what stories do we find connections? Where do our personal experiences lead us to resonate with a story?

Restoration to Wholeness

In these stories restorative actions are often taken beforehand by friends or by the community. Invite the group to consider the situations giving rise to the headlines or photos on the collage, as well as their personal experiences of brokenness. What restorative actions might be taken in order to prepare persons in broken circumstances to be restored to wholeness? What might the community do to offer the gift of belonging? Where have we witnessed the giving back of life or hope once thought to be lost?

Faith and Fear

Ask for a show of hands of those who agree or disagree with the following: Faith is not a vaccination against all that might come to us or even against us. Invite volunteers to respond as to why they agree or disagree. If they disagree, what medical analogy would they say does correspond to the experience of faith? Consider the comment of the priest at Lourdes that the greatest miracle he had ever seen was the faith of those who go away without a cure. What does the study writer mean when he says that healing and cure are not always the same?

Consider the stories again from the perspective of the fear engendered by Jesus' restorative actions. Why did Jesus' actions of healing, performing exorcisms, or restoring life or calm waters cause such great fear? Invite the group to name times today when fear has led persons, groups, or even nations down the path of more ominous directions or responses.

Live the Story

Invite the group to name persons, programs, incidents, or other aspects of life that might represent signs of ministries of reconciliation. List these on a large sheet of paper. Which of these signs might work to restore wholeness to the situations illustrated on the collage? Which might extend the open arms of inclusion to draw persons into community?

Ask the group to listen as you read aloud 1 Corinthians 12:12-27. Pray together in silence, considering where and who among us, within the body of Christ and in the world at large, are in need of restoration. What places within ourselves are in need of a healing touch? How can the faith community be Christ's instrument of healing and restoration of wholeness? What practices and disciplines do we need to nurture, as individuals and as a community, in order to prepare for the possibility of restoration and healing?

5. God's Character and Reign
Luke 11:1-13, 33-36, 37-54; 12:22-34, 35-48; 13:18-30; 14:7-24; 15:1-32; 16:19-31

Faith Focus
In the midst of a host of other realms making claims on our lives, the character of God and the present and future reign that God intends should transform how we live.

Before the Session
Gather drawing paper and crayons, as well as writing paper and pens or pencils.

Claim Your Story
Give participants drawing paper and crayons, and invite them to sketch out their childhood image of how God looked. Those reluctant to draw can use words, symbols, or phrases. Ask participants to hold up their rendition so that the group can view their collective images. Encourage volunteers to describe what they have depicted. Discuss how life experiences have shaped the image of God they carry now.

Ask participants to call out the name for God they use when they pray, and list these on a large sheet of paper. How does what we trust the character of God to be shape our choices about what we pray for? The study writer characterizes prayer as a conversation. What do we we bring to the conversation? What do we withhold?

Enter the Bible Story
Parables of Surprising Growth and Grace
The study writer compares parables with the understanding in Celtic spirituality of the "thin places" where the boundaries between heaven and earth seem to dissolve. In the study, the passages being considered are described as parables of surprising growth and grace. Ask participants to choose one of the following passages and read it silently: Luke 12:35-48; 13:18-30; 15:1-32. Then discuss: What are the surprises in the passage you read? What might we characterize as offensive or countercultural?

Invite the group to consider how the Gospel understanding of surprising growth relates to our obsession in the church with "church growth." If our churches expand to include large memberships, what would Luke say must also be a key feature of that growth, other than sheer numbers? In what ways must God's all-surpassing grace be demonstrated—for example, who would Luke say must be a target for our outreach, the focus of our inclusion?

The God We Encounter in Christ
Ask half the group to read Luke 16:19-31 and the other half to read Luke 11:37-54. Who in our time might parallel the rich man who ignores Lazarus? Who are the Lazaruses of our day? What is a contemporary version of the pious superficiality revealed by the Pharisees? How would you say our relationship with God is affected if we neglect the love and justice that exemplify the character of God?

Read aloud in unison the version of the Lord's Prayer found in Luke 11:1-4 and then Matthew 6:9-13. What differences do we hear? Compare the two versions of the prayer, using the passages as well as the information in the sidebar. How might our prayers and faith be shaped by our understanding of an all-inclusive God? A God-with-us, in our midst rather than in a distant heaven? Invite the group to respond to the other questions posed by the study writer about the implications the character of God has for our actions toward others, our practice of ethics and societal engagement, and the integration of our faith into all of life.

Preparing for God's Reign

Remind participants that the theme of preparation has already emerged in previous passages they studied. Where and in what ways in this session's passages does the emphasis on faithful stewardship emerge? Where do we see trust in God's providence? Point out that a practice in vogue today is the making of a bucket list—a list of those things a person wants to do before he or she "kicks the bucket." Invite participants to make, instead, a "treasure list" as suggested in the text—a list of those things they value most in life. Suggest that they reflect on the questions of how the things on the list come into play with the affirmations regarding the character of God and the nature of God's sovereign realm. If we are completely honest, how do our lives reflect those priorities—or not?

Live the Story

Invite the group, as the study writer suggests, to look back at the depiction of their childhood image of God that they created at the beginning of the session and answer the question in the text: How have those initial thoughts and perspectives been affirmed; been challenged; been the source of fresh perspective? On the other side of their drawing, invite them to add to or transform their image.

Pray together, beginning by inviting each participant to invoke a name for God that reflects in some way an aspect of the character of God they value highly. It might be the traditional "Our Father," or it might be "Creator God," "God of Justice," "God, my Rock," "Saving God," or any other name.

6. Costs and Joys of Discipleship
Luke 9:46-48, 57-62; 10:1-12, 17-20, 25-37, 38-42; 14:25-33; 18:18-30; 19:1-10

Faith Focus

The life and ministry of Jesus give discipleship a cruciform shape and calling. In the midst of the joys and costs of our choices, discipleship is revealed in our willingness to practice that cruciform following.

Before the Session

Reflect on the statement "Take up your cross and follow me." What are the choices and "detachments" that are particular to your life? From what are you called to turn away?

On a large sheet of paper, print the open-ended prompt "A disciple is . . ." and post it along with a felt-tipped marker. Obtain index cards and pens or pencils.

Claim Your Story

Ask participants to complete the open-ended prompt. Give each person an index card. Invite them to think of a time they made a choice involving discipleship and to write the costs of their choice on one side of the card and the joys on the other. On balance, did the scale tilt to one side or the other? Why? When and under what circumstances did you experience the costs and joys of discipleship inseparably joined?

Enter the Bible Story
Discipleship: What Are We Talking About?

Ask participants to name persons whose lives serve as embodiments of Christian discipleship. Look at what participants wrote in response to the open-ended prompt. Ask the group to scan the sidebar on page 61 and to name additional words or phrases and add those to the responses on the sheet.

How do we interpret the statement in the study that Jesus gives discipleship a cruciform shape and calling? Read aloud Luke 14:25-26, and ask participants to imagine that this biblical text is being read on Mother's Day or Father's Day. How might the congregation respond? Recall the list participants made in the last session of things they value. Which of the persons or things on that list represent the highest priorities in our lives? What would it mean to reorder these priorities in the light of the demands of discipleship? How do we balance the demands of love or commitment to vocation with what we may be called to do as disciples? What happens if they are in direct conflict?

Read aloud Luke 9:57-62. Complete the following: "I will follow you, Lord. But first, let me . . ." How is each of us called to practice our own particular cruciform following?

Discipleship: Disciplines for the Way

On a large sheet of paper, print the words "information" and "formation." How is it a formative discipline to keep your eyes set upon what is ahead? How might the discipline of humility alter some of the conflicts that are affecting our churches today? What form might humility take in your life, and how might it be formative of your faith?

Read the parable of the good Samaritan in Luke 10:25-37. Although the question posed by the young man was "Who is my neighbor?" Jesus turned the question around and asked the young man who acted as a neighbor. If love is what we are able to do with no thought of recompense, how does the practice of this discipline form us? In being formed, is it possible to be transformed? If so, how? Add the word "transformation" to the large sheet of paper.

Discipleship: Conflicts and Expectations

Read Luke 10:1-12, 17-20, naming the positive and negative expectations laid out in the passages. Consider Dietrich Bonhoeffer's decision that acting as a disciple required returning to Germany, with the cost of losing his life. What disciplines do we employ in evaluating how we respond to difficult issues? What cost are we willing to pay for our own cruciform following? How does the group respond to the suggestion that whatever you possess that you cannot give up possesses you? Like Zacchaeus, have you ever experienced joy in letting go of something close to your heart that may be getting in the way of the faithful life?

Examine the story of Mary and Martha (10:38-42). How do we prioritize the disciplines of discipleship? When is hospitality primary? When is listening? Respond to the following: "The grace and wisdom for a disciple is to know what time it is: to listen, to serve; to give up, to take on; to bring peace, to disturb what only masquerades as peace."

Live the Story

Invite participants to engage in the spiritual practice of examining the conscience as a form of prayerful discernment. First ask them to consider a choice your faith community is facing. Invite participants to find a comfortable sitting position, to close their eyes, and to breathe deeply for a few moments. Then ask the following, allowing time for silent reflection:

What anticipated costs are associated with this choice? What expected joys may be drawing us one way or the other?

Silently pray for wisdom and discernment in this choice. If time allows, repeat the process considering a personal choice.

7. Ascending and Descending Into Jerusalem
Luke 19:28–22:53

Faith Focus
As pilgrims, Christ prepares us to be a people of hope, even and especially in the most desperate of times.

Before the Session
As you prepare to lead the group, consider that in teaching, the destination frequently is secondary to the journey itself. Whether or not the group can detail the distinct features of Luke's rendering of Jesus' journey to Jerusalem is less important than the interactions and relationships persons form along the way—with one another and with the God of the journey. Obtain paper and pencils for the lifeline activity.

Claim Your Story
Invite the group to consider journeys they have experienced that they might have preferred deferring or avoiding. What are trips we fear because we don't know what lies ahead? What are other journeys where we know all too well what is in store for us? What are factors or considerations that help us to determine when such a journey must be made in order for healing to take place?

A pilgrimage takes us to a place or a person invested with special or holy meaning. Ask the group to consider in what ways they view life as a pilgrimage. When has a journey you would have preferred to avoid taken on the character of a pilgrimage?

Enter the Bible Story
Preparations for Pilgrims
What kinds of preparations are necessary when we go on an extended trip, such as a mission trip? What happens if a group embarks on a mission trip without preparing themselves to understand the complexities of a different culture or without prayer and Bible study? What if a group only views such a trip as a time to give, not an opportunity to receive?

Encourage participants to read over Luke 21:5-28, a passage the study writer suggests may reflect the voice and experience of Luke's community as it looks back at the destruction of Jerusalem in A.D. 70. In what ways does Jesus suggest the community prepare? In what ways are we called to prepare ourselves in these difficult times today? How does Christ prepare us to be a people of hope, rather than persons who prefer to avoid conflict at all costs? Ask the group to reflect on the questions in the text about Jesus' emphasis in verses 35-38 on traveling lightly. As we seek to be a pilgrim community, what kind of baggage may be weighing us down? In what ways might excess baggage impede the journey?

Confronting Fears

Ask participants to consider the passages cited in the text where fear seeks the shadows until there is no risk or breaks out in the open. The text notes that it is unclear what the Pharisees feared—the praise rendered to Jesus, the risk that any demonstration might get out of hand, or even fear that Jesus might be harmed by others. When have we experienced the fear that seeks to muffle voices of dissent? What is at risk when voices that seek to tell truth are silenced?

What was the risk to the rulers if they dealt with Jesus? Of whom were they afraid? When have we encountered fear in our faith pilgrimages? In what ways are we called upon to respond to those fears?

Passover Pilgrimage

Note that in Luke's account those who are rejoicing are Jesus' disciples, not the totality of the 50,000 or more people who were likely in Jerusalem for Passover. Briefly review with the group the sidebar on page 75 detailing the origins of the Passover in Exodus, noting that it centered in God's deliverance of the people from bondage. Then call attention to the four elements of the Passover meal itself. The study writer observes that the last element, the disciples' arguing over greatness, is the most critical element for discipleship. Does the group agree? What difference would it make if, as the study writer suggests, Luke 22:24-27 were required reading in every church dispute regarding the use of power and privilege? If servanthood is the disciple's path, how does that perspective shape our pilgrimages?

Live the Story

Distribute paper and pencils to the group. Say that one visual form of prayer is to make a spiritual lifeline that marks significant milestones in one's spiritual life. Ordinarily these lifelines are constructed as simple horizontal lines, with important events in one's faith journey penciled in on the line. For this exercise, however, invite participants to make an ascending and descending lifeline—a lifeline that illustrates the ups and downs they may have experienced in their spiritual lives.

Recall that the study writer notes that spiritually Jesus' ascent was marked by praise and expectation, while his descent was punctuated with conflict and betrayal. Ask the group to consider the questions in the study, then chart their lifeline on paper. Close with a prayer asking that God grant a renewed vision of hope for the pilgrimage of faith.

8. Closing—and Opening—the Gospel
Luke 22:54–24:53

Faith Focus
Out of the closures of passion and suffering arises the potential of resurrected and Spirit-filled openings to new life. So it can also be in our own lives.

Before the Session
Head one large sheet of paper with the words "Closures That Deaden." Print the following Scripture citations under the head: Luke 22:54-62; 22:63-65; 22:67-71; 23:1-7; 23:8-12; 23:13-24. On another sheet, put the words "Closures That Enliven" and print the following: Luke 22:62; 23:26-27; 23:34; 23:47; 24:6; 24:9-10; 24:13-35; 24:36-49. Get a loaf of bread to share in the closing—not as Communion but as a way of breaking open bread together as a community.

Claim Your Story
Invite participants to reflect on the questions the study writer poses about personal experiences of closure they may have recently faced or that are looming before them. If the closure is a job elimination or the death of a cherished loved one, it represents the termination of a pathway not chosen by the person and may represent a stiff challenge to one's faith. Even a long-anticipated retirement may engender ambivalent emotions. How might experiences of closure lead to new openings? How do we cope when only dead ends seem to be on the horizon?

Enter the Bible Story
Closures That Deaden and Closures That Open
Invite participants to choose one of the passages of Scripture from the large sheet of paper headed "Closures That Deaden" and one from the sheet headed "Closures That Enliven." Ask them to read the information in the text concerning the passages they chose, then also consider the following:

Closures That Deaden: In the passages, what are the factors that make the closure deadening? What, or who, is closed off, denied, or threatened? What emotions come in to play that contribute to death rather than life?

Closures That Enliven: In the passages, what are the factors that make the closure enlivening? What, or who, is opened up, affirmed, cathartic, revealed? What emotions come into play that contribute to life rather than death?

After allowing time for participants to reflect, consider each passage and invite response. If some passages were not chosen, look at them as a group. Who are the characters in these passages? Which of these characters evoke a sympathetic response from us? When have we responded as did Peter, closing ourselves off from the community? When have we acted as did Pilate, washing our hands of a situation we did not choose and will not engage? When have we just done as we were told, even in the face of injustice?

Invite the group to discuss personal experiences of closure and ways they may be similar to the ones related in the Scriptures.

Consider the places where Luke reveals that closings lead to openings. How does Jesus open doors from death into life, even as he hangs on the cross? How do Jesus' acts of forgiveness and remembering break open new life? How have participants experienced newness breaking in through being forgiven or acknowledged?

How is the risen Christ opened up to us in the empty tomb? How is the risen Christ opened up to us in Scripture? How is the risen Christ opened up to us in the breaking of the bread?

Opening to God's Future

The study observes that the closing narratives of Luke's Gospel leave any number of doors ajar—the invitation and choices thus pass from the characters on the page to those of us who are reading. What is the function of wondering in these stories? Invite the group to respond to what about the empty tomb engenders wondering in them. What blocks us from encountering Jesus as the Scripture is opened to us, or as the bread is broken in his name?

The study writer observes that to wonder at Jesus is not the same thing as following Jesus. The Gospel of Luke invites us to move from wonder into trust, from emotional and spiritual rushes into discipline and persistent following. In what ways does the information we gain when we engage with Scripture form us, opening us so that we may be transformed? In what ways would our life of faith look different if we take seriously what it means to be a disciple—to follow Jesus? What is the difference between wondering about Jesus and trusting in him?

Live the Story

Ask the group to respond to the following: "In Luke's Gospel, I was surprised by God in the story of . . ." "I experienced the expansive love and grace of God in the story of . . ." "I learned more about the practice of faith in . . ."

Pass around a loaf to share. As each person takes a piece of bread, invite participants to share a story or passage from this study when their hearts burned within them with the recognition of the presence of Jesus Christ. Pray that participants may be opened to the transforming power of God in Jesus Christ.